TABLE OF CONTENTS

Top 20 Test Taking Tips

1. Carefully follow all the test registration procedures
2. Know the test directions, duration, topics, question types, how many questions
3. Setup a flexible study schedule at least 3-4 weeks before test day
4. Study during the time of day you are most alert, relaxed, and stress free
5. Maximize your learning style; visual learner use visual study aids, auditory learner use auditory study aids
6. Focus on your weakest knowledge base
7. Find a study partner to review with and help clarify questions
8. Practice, practice, practice
9. Get a good night's sleep; don't try to cram the night before the test
10. Eat a well balanced meal
11. Know the exact physical location of the testing site; drive the route to the site prior to test day
12. Bring a set of ear plugs; the testing center could be noisy
13. Wear comfortable, loose fitting, layered clothing to the testing center; prepare for it to be either cold or hot during the test
14. Bring at least 2 current forms of ID to the testing center
15. Arrive to the test early; be prepared to wait and be patient
16. Eliminate the obviously wrong answer choices, then guess the first remaining choice
17. Pace yourself; don't rush, but keep working and move on if you get stuck
18. Maintain a positive attitude even if the test is going poorly
19. Keep your first answer unless you are positive it is wrong
20. Check your work, don't make a careless mistake

The Family

Family versus individual

A family is commonly considered a group of people that is related by birth, adoption, or marriage who reside together usually for the purpose of raising children. However, a family can refer to any group of individuals that live together in the same household even if they are not related by blood or legal ties. This means that an unmarried couple who is living together or even a pair of roommates may be considered a family.

A single individual, however, is the opposite of a family as it is a person who lives alone and therefore does not have to regularly interact with relatives or other individuals within the household.

Family structure

The four major types of family structures are nuclear, extended, single-parent, and blended and each of these structures are based on the idea that a family is a group of people who aid in the raising of the next generation.
- A nuclear family is the traditional concept of a family where there is a mother, father, and their children living in the same household.
- An extended family is an expansion of the nuclear family that includes the mother, father, and their children, as well as aunts, uncles, cousins, and grandparents.
- A single-parent structure is simply a family where one parent is the only one in the home caring for the children.
- A blended family, also known as a stepfamily, is when a parent marries or remarries when they already have their own children and there is a parent, stepparent, and one or more children living in the household.

Recent changes

The typical structure of families in the United States has changed drastically in recent years as the norm moves away from the traditional nuclear family towards the ever more common structure of the blended family. As more and more individuals divorce and remarry, blended families become much more common because children are being taken care of by both biological and stepparents more frequently. This increase in the number of blended families, which were virtually unheard of fifty to sixty years ago, has also led the structure of the blended family to be extended into two sub-structures, simple and complex, based on whether both parents have children or not. In a simple stepfamily only one of the individuals marrying has children, but the other does not and in a complex stepfamily both parents marrying have their own children before marriage.

Family stages

There are commonly 9 stages that a family can go through from beginning to end:
- The first stage, which is the single or bachelor stage, is where the individual is yet to be married and the family is not really a family, but rather a single individual.
- The second stage is the newly married couple stage where two individuals have just married, but do not have children yet.
- The third stage is the beginning of the three full nest stages where

- 5 -

the family has children and is attempting to raise them. Full nest stage I is where the youngest child is under 6.

- The fourth stage, full nest stage II, is where the youngest child is 6 or over,
- The fifth stage, full nest stage III, is the stage where an older married couple has dependent children.
- The empty nest I stage is where the head of the household in an older married couple is still in the labor force, but the couple has no children living with them.
- The empty nest II stage is the same as the empty nest I stage except that the head of the household has retired.
- The solitary survivor in labor force stage is when one of the couple has passed away and the survivor must continue to work to support him or herself.
- The final stage, the retired solitary survivor stage, is the same as the solitary survivor in labor force stage, except that the survivor has retired and there are no longer any individuals living in the household still in the labor force.

Purpose of family

The primary purpose of a family is to aid in the survival of the family and nurture the children of the family. Families allow individuals to survive more easily by dividing up the work and tasks necessary to survive by sharing those tasks, such as working and taking care of the home, with the rest of the family. Families also provide emotional support to the members of the family during times of high stress. The family aids in the nurturing of children by offering social and emotional interaction, protecting the children from potential danger, and educating the children in social norms and customs. The family also provides the basic necessities required, such as food, clothing, shelter, and play, for the basic physical development of the children in the household.

One of the most important functions a family provides is developing and educating the members of the family. Parents and grandparents pass their heritage and teachings of social norms and acceptable behavior to the children of the family through their customs, traditions, and ultimately their actions. Children learn about their heritage through the traditions of the family and also often learn lessons about the manner in which they are expected to behave by using the behavior of their parents and the rest of the household as a model for how the child should behave. Children also learn about the manner in which the world around them functions through the interactions of the members of the family with the world outside of the household. This allows the child to understand more complex types of social interaction such as what goods the family needs, where the family must go to fulfill those needs, and what is needed to acquire those necessities, such as how much money is required to purchase an item.

The following terms with regard to their importance in the development and education of family members:

- Behavioral modeling, when relating to how a child develops within a family structure, is the manner in which a child models their own behavior after the behavior of their parents and other people that interact with them. A child learns what behavior is socially acceptable by mimicking the behavior of the people around them.

- Consumer education is the process of teaching a person to understand the manner in which the marketplace works specifically in regards to the goods and services available, the suppliers of those goods and services, and the things to look for and look out for when searching for goods and services. These concepts are very important for a family member to learn how to protect themselves and survive in a consumer society.
- Heritage is simply anything that is inherited from one's ancestors such as traditions, customs, or even physical characteristics. The family acts as a medium to convey the traditions, customs, and social norms of the previous generation to the children that follow.

Healthy family roles

There are five major roles that are essential to the functioning of a family, which are providing necessities, development and education, emotional support, management of the family, and satisfying the needs of the married couple. Individuals within the family need to provide necessities by creating income so the family can be supplied with food, clothing, and shelter. Family members need to teach not only customs, but also skills that will help the members of the family successfully advance through school and eventually into a career. Families need to provide emotional support for other family members during times of high stress and the family needs someone to take a leadership role and handle issues such as managing finances and maintaining the roles essential to the family's survival. The married couple also

has their own needs, such as basic necessities, sexual needs, and basic emotional needs that need to be met for the family to continue functioning normally.

The following terms are important to keep in mind regarding family roles:

- A role is a series of social rights, behaviors, and obligations that are assigned to a particular individual. For example, a mother's role might be that of a provider as she is out in the workforce attempting to provide income for the family.
- Role confusion is when an individual is uncertain of what role or roles they should play in a particular situation. For example, a nurse might run into a patient whom she took care of previously while out grocery shopping and be unsure of whether to act in a formal, nurse to patient manner or in an informal, friendly manner.
- Role strain is when an individual is placed in a situation that carrying out the duties of a certain role will prevent the individual from fulfilling their obligations to another role. For example, a working mother might be both caregiver and provider and if her child becomes ill she cannot carry out both roles as she is forced to choose between working and caring for the sick child.

Married couples

The married couple, or in some cases simply the couple living together, make up the center of the family and therefore have a profound effect on the relationships and well-being of the family as a whole. If the marital couple is having difficulty in their relationship and the stress of those difficulties becomes apparent, the rest of the family will most likely exhibit signs of the same stress. For example, if the marital couple is consistently seen fighting, or even if they just become withdrawn after a fight has taken place, other members of the family may react to the stress of the married couple and become more withdrawn, upset, or even hostile. On the other hand, marital couples that are not experiencing marital difficulties and seem warm and affectionate will foster the same feelings of warmth and affection in the rest of the family.

Marriage

Marriage is a union, usually between two individuals, that is often held as a legally binding contract for the members of the union stating their intention to live together and aid each other in maintaining a family for the rest of their lives. Even though couples who simply live together in the same household can constitute a family under the commonly used definition, the institution of marriage offers a level of stability to the family structure that is not present when an unmarried couple makes up the center of the family. This added stability is primarily a result of the societal, religious, and governmental recognition of the institution of marriage that creates an expectation that the marriage and ultimately the family will remain intact. Although many married couples eventually separate and divorce, it is more difficult for any member of the marital couple to leave the family than it would be for a member of a couple that had no legal or societal obligation to remain together.

Divorce

Divorce is the termination of the union created by marriage before the death of any member of the union and it has a significant impact upon the stability of the family as a whole as well as affecting the relationships and well-being of the individual members of the family. Often when the marital couple decides to divorce, there has already been significant stress placed upon the entire family from the difficulties the marital couple has been experiencing. However, especially when children are involved, divorce can often lead to a great deal more stress being placed on the family and individuals within and outside the marital couple may become more withdrawn or hostile as the structure of the family changes. Divorce also allows both members of the marital couple to later remarry, as their legal obligation no longer exists, which can alter the family structure further by adding stepparents to the family.

Studies indicate that the age that a couple marries may have a significant impact on whether they remain married for an extended period. Individuals who marry before either member of the couple is 18 will often separate within a few years of their marriage. Individuals who are in the 18-25 range will separate less frequently than those who marry before 18, but are still at a very high risk for their marriage ending in divorce rather than death. Individuals who marry after they are both over 25 have a significantly lower risk of divorce than those who would marry at younger ages. Ultimately, statistics show that the risk of divorce seems to decrease as the age of each member of the couple at the time of the marriage increases.

There are many factors that may influence the risk of a marriage ending in divorce including income, education, religion, pregnancy before marriage, and whether the parents of the married couple are divorced. Couples who make over $50,000 a year are at a much lower risk of seeking a divorce than couples who make less than that amount. Couples that consist of well-educated individuals, who have graduated from high school and have at least some college background, also have a much lower risk of seeking a divorce than less educated individuals. Couples with no religious background or drastically different religious backgrounds have a much higher risk of divorce than couples that have religious backgrounds that do not conflict. Couples that have a baby prior to being married also have a higher risk of divorce than couples who have children after they are married. Individuals with parents who are divorced also have a higher risk of divorce than individuals from families that are intact.

Social and economic factors

Many social and economic factors can influence the overall functioning of a family. In fact, researchers use an index called the socioeconomic status or SES, to measure the ability of the family to function in a healthy fashion. The SES uses the educational background of the members of the family, the family's total income, and the skill, both actual and perceived, required by the occupations of the individuals who act as providers for the family to measure the family's ability to function. Individuals who are well educated tend to marry later in life, receive jobs with higher incomes, and have careers with a higher social status, which all add stability to the marriage and stability to the overall functioning of the family. Families that have a large amount of income are also less concerned with obtaining basic necessities, as the family consistently has the means to obtain them, and as a result there is often less stress throughout the family.

Communication

The two primary types of communication that members of a family use to communicate with one another are affective communication and instrumental communication. Affective communication is any communication where an individual demonstrates their feelings whether it is through facial expressions, motions, gestures, or even by stating their feelings outright. Instrumental communication is when an individual informs another member of the family of a piece of factual information that is necessary to carry out the normal day-to-day functions of the family such as a mother informing her child where he can find his or her socks. Families that use both types of communication usually function more effectively than families that use instrumental communication more often than affective communication.

Clear communication is when an individual states the information they are trying to convey outright and there can be no question as to the meaning of their statement. For example, if someone were to state "I am upset because Daniel is not home from the movies yet" that is an example of clear communication as there is no question that the individual making the statement is upset and they are specifically upset at Daniel for not being home. On the other hand, masked communication is when an individual states the information they are trying to convey in a vague and perhaps somewhat more confusing manner. For example, if someone were to state simply "I am upset" that would be an example of masked communication as there is no indication to the rest of the family as to exactly why the person is upset. As can be seen through these examples, clear communication is always more effective in conveying a particular piece of information than masked communication

Direct communication is when a person who is attempting to communicate a particular piece of information simply just tells that information to the person they want to receive the information. Indirect communication, on the other hand, is when the person communicating the information states the information, but not to anyone in particular. For example, if a parent told their child "Christine, we need to set the table" that is an example of direct communication as the parent is addressing the person they want to talk to directly. However, if the parent instead simply muttered out loud "we need to set the table" rather than saying it to someone in particular that would be an example of indirect communication. Direct communication is far more effective in carrying out the day-to-day functions necessary to maintain a family than indirect communication because various tasks can be assigned directly to a particular individual.

Families with individuals that use direct, clear communication, listen to the other members of the family, spend more time together communicating, respect each other's points of view, and pay attention to the more subtle forms of affective communication are the most effective. Each individual within the family, by informing the individuals that make up the family directly and concisely of the information they need to convey creates a much more effective form of communication than that which would be found in any other setting. If the individuals receiving the information listen to and respect their fellow family members and often more importantly make the time to listen to them in the first place, the communication between family members will become much stronger. Of

course, this communication can be strengthened even further if members of the family are careful to take note of emotional indicators that allow them to realize the feelings of another family member without that person having to actually express their feelings verbally.

Problem-solving steps

A well functioning family would first identify the problem itself and determine exactly what the cause of the problem is. The family would then come up with a list of solutions that could potentially solve the problem and then attempt to determine the benefits of each solution. After determining the benefits of each solution, the family would choose the solution that seemed to best solve the problem that they had encountered and then, after putting the solution into effect, monitor the solution to make sure that it actually solved the problem. Finally, the family would decide whether the solution worked or not to determine whether it was necessary to try something else. This entire process is important to the functioning of a family as it prevents problems from being misdiagnosed early on and prevents them from getting too far out of control.

Conflict

The causes of conflict within a relationship are too numerous to mention all of them, but some of the common causes include: setting expectations that are too high, not appreciating or respecting the other person in the relationship, not considering the feelings of the other person in the relationship, being afraid of showing affection or emotion, being over-dependent on the other member of the relationship, being inflexible, expecting the other member of the relationship to change, a lack of

- 10 -

effective communication, etc... Preventing conflict can be extremely difficult and preventing it altogether is virtually impossible, but avoiding some or all of these common sources can greatly reduce the number of conflicts that take place in any given relationship.

A family that is attempting to resolve a conflict can prevent the conflict from getting out of control and bring it closer to a successful resolution by following steps very similar to that of the basic problem-solving model. First, the family needs to attempt to identify the problem making sure to keep communication between the members of the family open, objective, and with as little hostility as possible. Once the problem is identified then the family needs to attempt to recognize the various positions that each member of the family has regarding the conflict while again attempting to keep hostility to a minimum. After each person involved in the conflict has made their position clear, the family needs to attempt to find a compromise that will work for everyone involved. Each step of the conflict resolution process requires that the people involved in the conflict remain as patient and as understanding as possible, which can often be extremely difficult especially when a solution or compromise cannot be determined immediately.

Social interaction

Outside social interaction is extremely important for every member of a family, regardless of age, as it offers an opportunity for each individual to improve their social skills, educate themselves about the world around them, and learn more about values that one might not learn from the family alone. This is especially true in the case of children as research shows that children who have regular outside social interaction, through things such as extracurricular activities, are less likely to rebel and cause problems and more likely to do better in school and relationships. Outside social interaction is also necessary for the children of a family to eventually leave the household and create a family of their own as they need to seek out their own relationships. Therefore, social interaction with individuals outside of the family is necessary not only for the fulfillment of the members of the family, but to continue the lifecycle of the family as well.

Human Development

Changing roles

Fifty to sixty years ago women were the primary caretakers of the family's children and in charge of maintaining the household while the men worked to provide for the family. This has changed, however, due to the drastic increase in the number of women entering the work force since that time, which is partially due to the fact that it has become progressively more difficult for families to live off of one income alone. Both members of the marital couple are often forced to work to provide for the family, which can make it difficult when trying to balance the responsibilities of caretaker and provider. Men, who were once the primary providers for the family, are still out in the workforce, but their spouses have joined them as well and both individuals have to find ways to make the time to care for the children of the family.

Nature versus nurture

The concept of nature vs. nurture is simply the idea that out of all of the traits that any given individual has, some are a result of their genetic heritage and some are a result of their environment. Nature in this context refers to any trait that an individual is born with and that they acquired through genes passed down from their parents. Nurture is in some ways seen as the opposite of nature as it refers to any trait that an individual learns from the environment around them. Nurture often refers to specifically the environment created by the parents of the child, but it can refer to any environmental condition that affects the development of that child. The concept of nature vs. nurture is important because it shows that individuals inherit some of their traits from their parents, but they also develop many of their traits from their environment.

Genetic and environmental traits

Some examples of traits that researchers have proven to be almost completely genetic and therefore linked to genes passed on from a child's parents to the child are eye color, blood type, most diseases and in most cases the risk of future diseases, vision and vision impairments, etc... Religion and language, on the other hand, are examples of traits that researchers have proven to be almost completely environmental. These traits are all linked to specific genes or to specific environmental factors, but most traits are actually a result of both environmental and genetic influence. Traits such as height, weight, and skin color are all examples of traits that are influenced by both an individual's genes and their environment.

Dvelopmental task concept

The developmental task concept is a theory of human development established by Robert Havinghurst that states that there are certain tasks that each individual needs to go through at certain points during their life to continue developing into a happy and successful adult. These tasks are separated into three groups by their causes and are tasks that are a result of physical maturation, personal causes, and societal pressures. A child learning to crawl is an example of a task that becomes necessary as the child matures physically while an individual learning basic first aid because they are interested in becoming an EMT is a personal cause. While a child that needs to learn how to behave appropriately in a store is an example of a task that would be presented as a result of a societal pressure.

The major age periods that Havinghurst identified for his developmental task concept are:

- Infancy and early childhood is the period from ages 0 to 5 and consists of tasks such as learning to walk and talk, learning to eat solid foods, and learning right from wrong.
- Middle childhood is the period of development from ages 6 to 12 and includes tasks such as learning to get along with others, learning moral values, and learning skills and knowledge required for day-to-day living.
- Adolescence is the period from ages 13 to 18 and requires tasks that include learning how to relate with members of the opposite sex, learning the social role of your gender in society, and preparing for life after childhood.
- Early adulthood is the period of life from ages 19 to 29 and is the age range where tasks such as starting a long-term relationship, finding a career, and starting a family are required.
- Middle adulthood is the period from ages 30 to 60 and includes tasks such as finding adult recreational activities, making achievements in your chosen career, and helping your teenage children to become healthy and happy adults.
- Later maturity is the period from ages 61 to the end of a person's life and consists of tasks such as adjusting to the death of a spouse, adjusting to the effects of old age, and finding people your own age to interact with.

Erik Erikson

Erik Erikson's theory of psychosocial development breaks the process of human development into eight stages that each person needs to pass during their life to continue functioning in a healthy fashion. The eight stages Erikson identified are infancy, younger years, early childhood, middle childhood, adolescence, early adulthood, middle adulthood, and later adulthood. During each of these stages, each individual has to overcome a particular obstacle to their development, which Erikson called a crisis, to be able to continue developing and face the crises of later stages. If an individual were not able to overcome one of the crises along the way, later crises would be more difficult to overcome as well. Erikson's theory also indicated that individuals who were unable to pass through a particular crisis successfully would likely encounter that same crisis again later in life.

- The first stage of Erikson's theory of psychosocial development is infancy and this stage covers the range of time from birth to 12 months. In this stage, the child is presented with the crisis of trust vs. mistrust. Even though everyone struggles with this crisis throughout their lives, the child needs to be able to realize the concept of trust and realize elements of certainty such as the fact that if the child's parents leave the room, they aren't going to abandon the child forever. If the child is unable to realize that there are certain things that can be left to trust because, for example, the child actually is abandoned, the child may become withdrawn and avoid interaction with the rest of society.

- The second stage of Erikson's theory of psychosocial development is the younger years stage, which covers the range of years from ages 1 to 3. In this stage, the child is faced with the crisis of autonomy vs. shame and doubt and is presented with the need to become independent and learn skills such as using the toilet without assistance. If the child is able to overcome this crisis, the child will gain a sense of self-pride that is necessary to continue fostering the child's growing need for independence as he or she gets older. If, however, the child is unable to overcome this crisis and cannot establish his or her own independence, the child will develop feelings of shame and doubt about the child's ability to function without assistance.
- The third stage of Erikson's theory of psychosocial development is the early childhood stage, which covers the range of time from ages 3 to 5. In this stage, the child is faced with the crisis of initiative vs. guilt and is presented with the need to discover the ambition necessary to continue functioning independently and ultimately a sense of the person the child wants to become in the future. This stage is strongly linked with the moral development of the child as he or she begins to use make-believe play to explore the kind of person he or she wants to become. If the child is unable to explore their ambitions or is expected to function with too much self-control the child will develop feelings of guilt as the child begins to see their

- ambitions, dreams, and goals as unattainable or inappropriate.
- The fourth stage of Erikson's theory of psychosocial development is the middle childhood stage, which covers ages 6 to 10. In this stage, the child is faced with the crisis of industry vs. inferiority and is presented with the need to develop the ability to complete productive tasks, such as schoolwork, and work together in groups with other people. If the child is unable to learn how to work effectively, either alone or in a group, the child will develop a sense of inferiority as a result of their inability to complete the tasks set before them that the child's peers are capable of completing. For example, if a child is regularly unable to complete their homework because the child does not understand the material while the rest of the child's peers are not having difficulty, this can lead the child to develop a sense of inferiority.
- The fifth stage of Erikson's theory of psychosocial development is the adolescence stage, which covers ages 11 to 18. In this stage, the child is faced with the crisis of identity vs. role confusion where the child attempts to find his or her place in society and determine his or her future goals and the skills and values necessary to achieve those goals. It is also at this stage that the child becomes more aware of how the people around the child perceive him or her and begins to become concerned with those perceptions. If the child is unable to determine what future goals he or she is

interested in pursuing, it can lead to confusion about what roles the child will play once the child reaches adulthood.

- The sixth stage of Erikson's theory of psychosocial development is the early adulthood stage, which covers ages 18 to 34. In this stage, the young adult is concerned with the crisis of intimacy vs. isolation where the individual needs to begin establishing intimate relationships with others. If the adult is unable to form intimate relationships with other individuals, perhaps because of disappointments regarding relationships earlier in life, the individual will become more withdrawn and isolate themselves from others. Isolation can prove to be a dangerous problem to the development of a healthy adult as it not only prevents the individual from forming lasting relationships, but the lack of social interaction can lead to severe personality flaws, which may hinder any future attempts at developing relationships later in life.

- The seventh stage of Erikson's theory of psychosocial development is the middle adulthood stage and occurs between ages 35 to 60. In this stage, the adult becomes aware of the crisis of generativity vs. stagnation where the individual is concerned with continuing their genetic line before it is too late. Generativity refers to the ability to produce offspring and then nurture, guide, and prepare that offspring for future life. At the same time, however, generativity in this context also refers to any act that gives something of value,

such as teaching children how to read, to the next generation. If an individual is unable to contribute to the next generation in some form or another, the individual will feel a sense of failure that is a result of stagnation, which is simply a lack of accomplishment.

- The last stage of Erikson's eight stages of psychosocial development is the later adulthood stage, which is the period starting at age 60 that goes on to the end of the individual's life. In the later adulthood stage, the individual is confronted with the crisis of ego integrity vs. despair where the adult begins to examine the course of his or her life and ultimately the kind of person that he or she has been over the years. If the adult feels that he or she has had a meaningful life and has accomplished something during it, this will lead to a strong sense of integrity. However, if the adult is unhappy with the way that the individual acted during his or her life, they will fall into a sense of despair as the individual begins to fear death and the absolute end of any chance of achieving anything further.

Jean Piaget

Jean Piaget's theory of cognitive development theorizes that a child will learn more effectively if the child is allowed to actively adapt to the world around them through their own play and exploration rather than being taught skills and knowledge by other people. Piaget's theory suggests that during a child's development there are four major stages that the child will go through as they begin to acquire new skills that will

- 15 -

aid their ability to learn and process information on their own. The four stages that Piaget identifies are the sensorimotor stage, which lasts from ages 0 to 2, the preoperational stage for ages 2 to 7, the concrete operational stage for ages 7 to 11, and the formal operational stage for ages 11 and onward. Piaget's theory is important to the study of child development as it was the first theory that actually recognized the concept that children can actively and effectively learn on their own rather than having to gain knowledge from simply being taught by another person.

- The first stage of Piaget's theory of cognitive development, the sensorimotor stage, lasts from birth to age 2 and is the period where a child uses their senses of sight, hearing, and touch to learn about and explore elements of the world around them. Through a combination of these senses, a child is able to discover new ways of solving simple problems such as how to move their hands to drop a block into a bucket and removing it again or using their eyes to find an object or person that has been hidden. As a result, it is also at this stage that the child begins to develop their hand-eye coordination and an ability to reason out a method of achieving any given goal.
- The second stage of Piaget's theory of cognitive development, the preoperational stage, lasts from ages 2 to 7 and is the stage where children begin to use words, symbols, and pictures to describe what they have discovered about particular elements of the world around them. This stage is where children begin to develop an understanding of language and

can focus their attention on a particular subject or object rather than everything going on at once. However, Piaget theorized that children at this stage of development also have a faulty sense of logic when attempting to understand certain concepts such as volume, mass, and number when some element of what they perceived was changed. For example, if a liquid was poured into a tall container and than an equal amount of liquid was poured into a smaller, but wider container, the children would believe that the taller container contained more liquid even though this obviously was not the case.

- The third stage of Piaget's theory of cognitive development, the concrete operational stage, which takes place between ages 7 and 11, is the stage where a child's thinking becomes more logical regarding concrete concepts. For example, in this stage children are now capable of understanding concepts of mass, volume, and number and are able to realize that two containers of different shapes that each have the same amount of liquid poured into them still contain the same amount of liquid. The child will also begin to learn how to identify and organize objects according to their shape, size, color, and so on. The child, however, will still not be able to understand more abstract concepts, such as what you might find in calculus or algebra, until they reach the formal operational stage of development.
- The fourth and final stage of Piaget's theory of cognitive development, the formal

- 16 -

operational stage, starts at age 11 and continues until the end of the individual's life. This stage is where an individual begins to understand more abstract concepts and develops a logical way of thinking about those concepts. In other words, the individual begins to understand ideas that are less concrete or absolute and cannot necessarily be backed up by physical evidence or observation such as morality, advanced mathematics, and a person's state of being. It is also within this stage of development that individuals become able to understand all of the variables in a problem and are able to determine most if not all of the possible solutions to the problem rather than just the solutions that are most obvious. This stage is never truly completed, but rather continues throughout a person's life as the individual continues to develop and improve on their ability to think abstractly.

Later researchers have challenged Piaget's theory of cognitive development because studies indicate that Piaget may have underestimated the abilities of younger children to learn and understand various concepts. Piaget's theory indicates that younger children are unable to understand certain concrete and abstract thoughts early within their development even if another individual taught the child. However, this has actually been disproved as research shows that children of a young age can actually be taught how to handle and understand problems that Piaget believed only older children would be able to comprehend. Researchers have also challenged Piaget's theory because studies indicate that if a younger child is

given a task like one an older child might receive, but the difficulty of the task is adjusted to compensate for age, the child would actually be able to more effectively understand the concept. Piaget's theory is still important because it presents the importance of active learning in a child's development, but it also ignores many of the benefits of adult teaching.

Abraham Maslow

Abraham Maslow originally theorized that there were five types of human needs that form a sort of pyramid if they are arranged in order of their importance. Maslow also stated that no individual would be able to focus on the upper layers of the pyramid until they were able to meet the needs presented at the layers below first.

- The first layer of the pyramid is the layer that contains the physiological needs, which are the basic needs required for the individual's survival such as food, water, breathable air, sleep, etc...
- The second layer of the pyramid is the layer that contains the safety needs, which are the elements that the individual needs to feel a sense of security such as having a job, good health, and a safe place to live.
- The third layer of the pyramid is the layer that contains the love and belonging needs, which is the basic need to form social relationships such as those with friends, family, and intimate loved ones.
- The fourth layer of the five layers of the pyramid that makes up Maslow's hierarchy of human needs is the esteem layer, which contains the individual's need to respect him or herself and others

- 17 -

as well as the need to be respected and accepted by others.

- The fifth and top layer of the pyramid is the self-actuation layer of the pyramid and contains the individual's need for morality, creativity, and trust. Maslow theorized that individuals could survive without reaching the later levels of the pyramid, but they would feel a sense of anxiousness if the needs of the later levels were not met. Maslow also believed that individuals who reached the later levels of the pyramid did not receive any tangible benefit from meeting the needs of those layers other than a feeling of fulfillment and the motivation to fulfill needs higher on the pyramid.

Maslow later added two additional layers above the self-actuation layer of the pyramid, which are the cognitive layer and the aesthetic layer.

- The cognitive layer is the layer that contains an individual's need to acquire and ultimately understand both abstract and concrete knowledge.
- The aesthetic layer, which became the final layer in later versions of the pyramid, is the layer that presents the individual's need to discover, create, and experience beauty and art.

Maslow also later theorized that if an individual was unable to meet the needs of the any given layer of the pyramid that those needs could become neurotic needs, which are compulsions that if satisfied would not aid in the individual's health and growth in any fashion.

Intervention and giftedness

Early childhood intervention is the process by which children who are experiencing developmental difficulties or showing signs of difficulties are diagnosed and treated as early as possible to allow them to continue developing in the best manner that the child can. Early childhood intervention services usually take place before the child reaches school age because studies indicate that the earlier a child who is experiencing difficulties receives special education, the more effective that education will ultimately be.

Children who possess intellectual giftedness are children that are born with a significantly higher than average IQ and are capable of learning concepts and information much more quickly than other children of their age. Even though intellectual giftedness is an asset to the child, the child often requires education that is adjusted for the speed that the child can learn at or the child will become bored, frustrated, isolated, and actually even begin to underachieve.

Substance abuse

Substance abuse is a disorder where an individual begins to overuse or becomes dependent upon a particular drug or a group of drugs that ultimately has a negative impact on the health of the individual. Substance abuse, especially when the individual using the drug becomes addicted or dependent on the drug, can affect the individual's ability to interact both socially and physically, and abilities such as their ability to communicate intelligibly with other people or even to complete relatively simple tasks can be severely hindered. Once an individual becomes chemically dependent on a particular drug, there body actually develops a physical need for

- 18 -

the drug and the individual will experience the effects of withdrawal if they are unable to meet that need. However, substance abuse not only affects a person by causing health problems, but also can severely hinder an individual's ability for social development, as the individual often has difficulty improving on social skills due to his or her inability to control behavior, actions, and even basic speech.

Teenage pregnancy

Teenage pregnancy, which can be defined as the act of a woman expecting a child prior to her 20th birthday or in some areas prior to her being considered a legal adult, can have a large number of physical, social, economic, and psychological effects. Studies show that women who become pregnant as teenagers have a significantly higher chance of giving birth to the child prematurely, a higher risk of the child being born at an unhealthy weight, and a higher risk of complications during pregnancy, especially when the mother is under age 15. It has also been shown that teenage mothers are more likely to drop out of high school and even more likely never to finish college, which can make it much more difficult for a teenage mother to find a job, especially if she is the sole caretaker of the child. Children born to teenage mothers have also been shown to be at higher risk for behavioral problems and often have more difficulty functioning in school.

The two primary ways that the risk of teenage pregnancy can be reduced are through the promotion of contraceptive use or abstinence and the promotion of social interaction between the teenager and her parents. The best way to reduce the risk of teenage pregnancy is certainly not to have intercourse at all, but the use of a contraceptive, even though it does not guarantee that a teenager will not become pregnant, can greatly reduce the chances of pregnancy when used correctly. Studies have also shown that teenagers that have regular open communication with their parents are more likely to wait to have intercourse until later in their lives. However, regardless of what precautions are used, the risk of teenage pregnancy cannot be eliminated completely as there is always the risk of contraceptives failing or the risk that the teenager may be the victim of a rape.

The most important thing for a young mother to continue functioning and raise her child in a healthy fashion is that she is able to maintain a stable and effective support system both before and after the child is born. Studies have shown that most of the physical effects that teenage pregnancy has upon the child, when the mother becomes pregnant at age 15 or older, are a result of malnutrition and poor prenatal care. Both of these factors can be greatly reduced or eliminated if the young mother has help from parents or outside resources that teach her what to eat and where to get appropriate care. A strong support system is also essential in aiding the mother financially and in actually raising the child as teenage parents almost always lack the resources and the life experience necessary to both supply and care for the child.

Teenage suicide

There are a large number of factors that can increase the risk of a teenager committing suicide, but studies indicate that the teenager's history, emotional and physical health, social pressures, and access to the equipment necessary to carry out the suicide are the most likely to have a role. If the teenager has attempted to commit suicide previously, has a history of drug or alcohol abuse, has a history of depression or other mental illness, or another member of his or her family has committed suicide or been abused, the teenager's risk of suicide increases. Physical illness, religious or cultural pressures, and other suicides in the community can also lead to an increased risk of suicide. Finally, if the teenager has access to guns, knives, drugs, or any other means of taking his or her own life, the teenager may be at heightened risk for suicide as well.

Teenage suicide can be difficult to prevent, but identifying the risk factors and attempting to minimize their effects before they are allowed to escalate is the most effective way to prevent teenage suicide. Teenagers that do not have access to the instruments necessary to easily commit suicide, but have access to facilities for both mental and physical health and support that promotes the use of such facilities, and overall have strong family, societal, and religious support are much less likely to commit suicide. Teenagers who have been taught methods of solving problems and conflicts in a non-violent fashion by their parents or teachers have also been shown to be at a much lower risk of suicide as well.

the other hand, activities that aid in the completion of goals that are less essential should be given a lower priority. This system allows an individual to rank goals and the corresponding activities that lead to their completion based on how essential they are to the individual or the organization.

Goals versus decision-making

- A goal is a particular purpose that an individual or group of individuals wishes to achieve in the near or distant future. For example, in a corporate setting, a goal might be to achieve a certain amount of sales in the next quarter while in a family setting a goal might be to find a job for a teenager in the family before summer ends.
- Decision-making is the process by which an individual or group of individuals attempts to determine the best option from a group of possible opinions and/or actions usually for the purpose of achieving a particular goal. For example, a young couple may be looking for a new home and, as they visit each house for sale, they may make a list of all the advantages and disadvantages of living in each house to help them decide which house to buy.

Goal-setting

Goal-setting is important because it allows an individual or organization to identify what they wish to accomplish and determine the best way to accomplish those objectives. Goal-setting also usually implies setting a particular timeframe in which the goal should be achieved. The combination of the individual or organization knowing what goals they are

striving for and that those goals need to be completed in a set amount of time aids in motivating the efforts of each individual involved towards that ultimate objective. Goals also give the individual or organization a means of measuring the amount of effort, or the lack thereof, that each individual puts into obtaining those goals. In a family or corporate setting, goals can give the organization a means of measuring its success as well, which can be important when attempting to determine what actions the organization needs to take in the future.

An individual or organization that is attempting to set a goal can follow the common management mnemonic SMART to make sure that their goal is well-defined, valid, and useful when attempting to measure success and motivate the organization as a whole. SMART, when relating to goals, usually refers to specific, measurable, achievable, relevant, and time-related. Goals need to be specific and well-defined, have some way of being measured in an accurate fashion, be achievable rather than unattainable and ridiculous, and relevant to the tasks that need to be completed for the success of the organization. The individual or organization should also decide upon a set amount of time that the goal should be completed in to make sure that it is achieved in a timely fashion and that it can be compared to other goals in the future.

Goal validity examples

- *A manager of a local retailer, that usually does somewhere between $35,000 and $60,000 a week, decided that his or her store should set a goal of making $50,000 in sales a week each week for the month of November. This is a completely valid goal as the goal is* very well-defined, it can be measured by examining the amount of sales the store has done each week, and the goal is achievable as $50,000 is within the store's normal sales range. The goal is also relevant to the store's ability to make a profit and there is a set amount of time that the goal must be achieved in.

- *A mother with a son who is having difficulty in school has decided that her son needs to improve his grades.* This example is not a valid goal as the goal is not well-defined, there is a manner of measuring the goal, but there is no mention of what is a satisfactory improvement in the son's grades, and there is no set timeframe for the goal to be completed in. The goal may be achievable and is certainly relevant to the success of the child, but it is not well-defined enough to be an effective goal.

Achieving goals

Many internal and external factors can have an effect on whether or not an individual or organization is able to achieve a particular goal. However, the most important thing for an individual or organization to keep in mind, regardless of the situation, is that there is a strong need to remain focused on the goal and the appropriate way to achieve that goal. This means that if a goal is important to the success of the individual, or the organization as a whole, it is important that every possible effort is placed into achieving that goal. Any other goals that might be less important or irrelevant should not be allowed to distract the individual or the organization from the primary goal and these secondary goals should ultimately be ignored until the

primary goal is achieved. It is also necessary that the individual or each individual within the organization can continue to recognize that the goal is achievable so no one gives up before the goal is actually reached.

Identifying and defining the goals that a family needs or wishes to accomplish and the moral values that the family needs to uphold is extremely important prior to any decision as it offers a guide as to what options are unacceptable before an incorrect choice is made. By identifying well-defined goals that the family wants to achieve in the future, the family can choose the options that appear to move the family closer towards the ultimate achievement of those goals. Defining the family's moral values outright is also important as it aids in eliminating choices that might be directly opposed to what the family considers correct and ethical.

Decision-making process

The primary reason that the decision-making process is important is because understanding the process can aid in the discovery of a future rational and reasonable course of action when presented with a decision that needs to be made. Each individual has a different perspective and therefore a different way of coming to a particular decision, but through a combination of intuition, knowledge, and an understanding of how the process works, a decision that is more suited for the goals of a particular individual or group can be made. A well thought out method of decision-making consists of identifying the decision that needs to be made, identifying the benefits of each choice relating to that decision, identifying the potential drawbacks of making each choice relating to that decision, and finally actually making a choice. An individual or organization by

- 23 -

understanding what needs to be identified at each stage of the decision-making process will be able to make a more informed decision that will be more likely to lead towards a particular goal.

Decision-making pitfalls

Some of the most common pitfalls that need to be avoided when attempting to make a well-informed decision are entering the decision-making process with a preconceived notion that the individual is unwilling to abandon, allowing peer pressure to influence a decision, and over-generalizing. Entering the decision-making process with a prejudice against a particular idea or source of information or with an inappropriate bias towards a particular choice will often lead to the individual or group choosing an option that is not the best or most logical of the choices available. Outside sources should be used to gather information about the decision that needs to be made, but no single source should be allowed to force or pressure the individuals involved in making the decision into choosing a particular choice. Finally, the overuse of generalizations, stereotypes, and attempts to attribute effects to causes that may not have any logical link will often lead to a decision being made that may not be the best course of action.

Decision-making techniques

An individual that is attempting to make a well-informed decision will often attempt to gather as much information as possible from as many reliable sources as possible, list the advantages and disadvantages of each choice, and then compare each choice with each other. In an employment or business situation where finances are involved, an individual may use a mathematical approach and

calculate exactly how much money each job choice or each potential new product could offer and how much it might cost the individual if something goes wrong. A mathematical approach, when it is possible to use one, can be an extremely sound strategy when attempting to determine which choice is more appropriate. However, many individuals do not make well-informed decisions and they may rely on random chance such as flipping a coin, on the opinions or pressure of the individual's peers, or rely heavily on information from unreliable sources such as a high school student's web page.

Organizational decision-making

Some of the most common decision-making strategies that a business or other organization might use when attempting to make a decision are the Pareto analysis system, a cost/benefit analysis strategy, a force field analysis strategy, a grid analysis strategy, and a scenario analysis strategy. Each business or other type of organization will usually choose the system that best suits the kind of decision that they are attempting to make as each strategy has its own advantages and disadvantages. For example, a Pareto analysis system can be useful when an organization is attempting to handle a particular group of problems and it is obvious that a particular small group of causes is responsible for most of the problems that the organization is having. However, a Pareto analysis system will not work as well, if at all, in situations where there are a large number of problems caused by completely unrelated factors.

Pareto analysis

Basically, the Pareto analysis system is a decision-making model that assumes that

- 24 -

approximately 80% of the benefits that an organization receives from a particular task are a result of 20% of the effort that the various individuals within the organization put into the task. It also assumes that 80% of the problems that the organization is faced with are produced by approximately 20% of the factors that may be causing them. The first step necessary for the Pareto analysis system is to list all of the problems that need to be addressed or the choices that are available. Next, each of those problems or choices needs to be grouped so that the choices that offer similar benefits or are factors that are leading to larger similar problems are grouped together. Each group is then given a score based on how much that group affects the overall benefit that the organization is attempting to achieve or the overall problem that the organization is attempting to solve.

Cost/benefit analysis

Cost/benefit analysis is a decision-making strategy that examines the total estimated cost of each option that is available, the total estimated benefit of each option available, and then compares the cost with the benefit to see if the benefits of the option outweigh the cost. Usually, a cost/benefit analysis refers to the financial cost and benefit of a particular decision, but it can actually be used in any situation where the use of resources is involved. For example, if a corporation has two clothing materials, A and B, that both cost the same, but material B can be used more efficiently, the cost/benefit analysis would show that material B is the best choice as it offers the most clothing for the least amount of material. Cost/benefit analysis can be extremely useful when attempting to decide which option will have the greatest benefit. However, this method also relies heavily on estimation so there may be instances where it is not as accurate as other methods.

Force field analysis

Force field analysis is a decision-making strategy that attempts to examine all of the factors that affect a particular situation and identify those factors as either aiding the organization in achieving a goal or ultimately causing the organization to fail. Basically, it is the process of identifying and listing which factors involved with each option are helping the organization and which ones are actually hurting the organization. The first step of the force field analysis strategy is to make a list of all of the factors involved with a particular option and identify them as either aiding the organization in moving towards a particular goal or hindering the organization's movement towards that goal. Each factor is then given a rating on a scale of 1 to 5 with 1 being the weakest and 5 being the strongest. If the forces that hinder the organization are stronger overall, the option is probably not realistic, however if the forces that aid the organization are stronger, then the option may prove beneficial.

Grid analysis

Grid analysis is a decision-making strategy that takes all of the factors involved with each option, rates each factor, and then weights each factor based on their importance to the decision as a whole. For example, if the owner of a clothing factory had three materials and was attempting to decide which material would provide the most profit, the owner might consider each material's cost, how much material is wasted, and how difficult each material is to use. The owner would then use a set scale, such as from 0 to 5 with 0 being the most expensive or wasteful and 5 being the least, and rate the cost, waste, and difficulty of use for each material. The owner would then assign each factor a weight based on the effect the factor has on the overall profit, using a similar scale, and then get a weighted score by multiplying the weight by the rating that each factor received. The material with the highest total score would be the best option.

Scenario analysis

The scenario analysis strategy is a decision-making method where an individual or organization attempts to use their experience, knowledge, and intuition to predict what kind of situations may arise from each option if that option were chosen. In other words, the scenario analysis strategy is where the decision-maker attempts to determine all of the possible outcomes of a particular choice and what effect each outcome might have on the organization or individual as a whole if that choice was made. In some instances, especially in a business setting, each of these potential outcomes might be assigned a score based on how likely it is that that scenario will actually occur. However, regardless of whether the potential outcomes receive a score or not, it is impossible for an individual or organization to arrive at every possible outcome that might occur and accurately predicting what events are most likely to occur in the future can be extremely difficult.

Resources

A resource is simply anything that can be used to aid an individual or organization in either the daily functioning of the individual or organization or aid in the achievement of a particular goal. The four primary types of resources are land and natural resources, labor resources, capital and capital goods, and information resources.

- Land and natural resources include anything that comes from the environment such as water, oil, the land itself, soil, etc…
- Labor resources are the actual effort that various people involved in an organization put into a particular project towards the goal of completing that project.
- Capital and capital goods are any financial and human-made resources such as money, tools and equipment, buildings and houses, or anything else that is man-made.
- Information resources are any resources that allow an individual or organization to find and put to use knowledge that might help in achieving a particular goal.

Determining resources

An individual or organization that is attempting to assess if there are enough resources available for a particular project may want to start by determining exactly what the project consists of and attempt to research how much the project will cost in time and money. After the individual or organization has developed a basic outline of what the project needs, an inventory of which resources are readily available should be conducted. This inventory would include noting resources such as how much money is available, how many people are available to work on the project, what kind of equipment is available to complete the project, and is there enough information regarding the project available for the workers to complete the project. If the

- 26 -

individual or organization determines that the resources necessary to complete the project are not available then the project is not realistic based on the resources that the individual or organization currently has.

A family that is attempting to determine the status of its financial resources should start by collecting all of the financial records that the family has available from each source of income. The family should then attempt to determine and list all of its assets including the amount of cash the family has on hand and the amount of cash the family could get if they sold off any stocks, bonds, mutual funds, property that the family owns, etc... After adding up all of the on hand assets and potential assets that the family has available, the family should then list all of the loans, unpaid bills, balances due, and other liabilities the family needs to pay and add them together to get the family's total amount of liability. The family can then get an idea of their financial standing by subtracting their estimated total liability from their estimated total assets giving them a good estimation of their net worth.

Using resources

Land resources can be used as locations for homes, businesses, or even searching for other natural resources located on that land such as oil, minerals, soil that can be used for planting, water for drinking and fishing, etc... Examples of people who might be considered as labor resources are marketers who determine the best way to sell a particular product, salespeople who sell a particular product to the consumer, the factory workers who actually assemble that product, and anyone else who actually aids in achieving the end goal. Capital refers specifically to money, but capital goods,

such as in a factory setting, can be the machinery that turns the raw goods into the end product. Information resources may be books or online sites that can be used to learn how to construct a better product or how to better manage a particular organization. All of these resources can be used in a variety of ways and most projects actually require a combination of different types of resources.

Non-financial resources

Non-financial resources, or resources that are not cash or can not be sold outright and turned into cash, can be extremely useful to a family that is experiencing financial problems. Even though non-financial resources are not actually cash or property that can be sold, they can often be used to produce income or reduce costs that the family is experiencing. For example, even though a family may not want to sell their house outright, and they obviously can't logistically sell just one room in their home, they can still rent out a room to make additional money. A family who has a seamstress or a carpenter as a member of the family might also be able to lower the family's costs by mending the family's clothing instead of throwing it away or making necessary repairs to the family home without paying for labor. Any skill that a family member possesses can cut the family's costs and any service the family can offer can act as a way of gathering additional income.

Change management

Change management is the process by which an organization attempts to modify a particular aspect of how the organization operates with as little harm to the organization as possible. In most cases, an organization makes these operational changes either to adapt to changes in society or to improve the manner in which the organization operates overall. Change management is important as almost everything around us is constantly changing, but many individuals have difficulty adapting to social, economic, or other changes despite how important making these changes might be. Organizations that want to continue functioning need to change in order to continue working with the world around them as it continues to change. Change management is simply the process that each organization uses to implement the changes that are necessary without putting too much unnecessary stress upon the members of the organization.

Change strategies

There are three major types of strategies that an organization might use when attempting to make changes in the way an organization functions overall. The three types of strategies are the empirical-rational strategy, the normative-reeducative strategy, and the power-coercive strategy. Each strategy has its own advantages and disadvantages and which strategy an organization chooses is usually based on how much the organization needs to change and what resources are available to relieve problems that may be caused by particular changes. Which strategy an organization uses may also be based heavily on how much time is available to make the changes and how great a risk there is of members of the organization rejecting the change and refusing to adapt.

- The empirical-rational strategy of managing change assumes that people are ultimately interested in their own well being and will more quickly accept changes if

they understand that those changes offer some sort of benefit. In other words, this strategy of managing change relies on either offering an incentive to the members of the organization to take part in some sort of change or convincing the members of the organization that the change will benefit them in some fashion. For example, if the board of directors of a particular company realized that the company's competitors had employees that were performing more effectively, because their employees had more education, the board might decide to use an empirical-rational strategy to encourage employees to go back to school. The company, by offering perhaps to pay for additional schooling and/or offering promotions, raises, or other incentives might be able to get some or most of their employees to seek out further education and return to the company better trained.

- The normative-reeducative strategy of managing change relies heavily on peer pressure to bring about the changes that an organization needs. Basically, this strategy assumes that people rely heavily on social interaction and therefore will normally behave according to the expectations of the rest of society. Using this assumption, an organization can institute new changes by slowly redefining aspects of the organization's culture and each individual will then begin to accept the changes as social norms. For example, if the board of directors of a retail chain begins to realize that customer service is becoming a more

- 28 -

important marketing point than price, the directors may attempt to use a normative-reeducative strategy. The company can slowly begin altering the behavior that is deemed socially acceptable by the employees by placing posters in the break room suggesting the importance of customer service, addressing the appropriate way to treat customers at meetings and performance reviews, and training new employees in good customer service tactics.

- The power-coercive strategy of managing change assumes that people will usually listen to authority figures and do as they are told. This strategy works simply by preventing the members of the organization from choosing any option other than the path that the manager wants them to follow because it is made clear that there are no other options available to them. If an individual still refuses to accept the changes that the organization has decided upon, the organization might punish the individual for not complying. For example, if a child is doing poorly in school because he is spending too much time watching television, the child's mother might simply turn off the TV and tell her child to do his homework. If the child then turns the television back on, his mother might send him to his room and ground him for a week as punishment for disobeying.

The empirical-rational strategy is very effective when an organization has the resources available to offer the incentives necessary to make the changes more palatable or if the changes have an

obvious benefit to the individuals who need to implement the change. However, it is much less effective when the organization lacks the resources to give incentives substantial enough to sway the members of the organization or the changes do not seem beneficial on the surface. The normative-reeducative strategy is useful when the managers and workers of the organization have a strong relationship and there is a lot of time available to implement the changes, however, this strategy is much less effective when there is limited time available or relations between management and staff are strained. The power-coercive strategy is particularly useful in situations where time is limited and the threat to the organization or individual is more serious, however, it often can promote unrest amongst members of the organization especially in organizations that allow more individual freedoms.

Consumer Economics

Consumer rights

Consumer rights are a series of protections, usually guaranteed by law, which protect individuals from being taken advantage of in the marketplace. In the United States, there is a countless number of state and federal laws that establish these rights and the consumer affairs departments of the various states, the Federal Trade Commission, and the U.S. Justice Department enforce these laws. Some examples of federal acts that have guaranteed certain rights to consumers are the Equal Credit Opportunity Act, the Fair Housing Act, the Fair Credit Reporting Act, the Fair Debt Collection Practices Act, and the Truth in Lending Act. All of these federal acts and state laws are important because they help prevent consumers from wasting their finances by spending them on products that were sold to them using less than ethical business practices. Some of these acts also protect the consumer from being discriminated against by businesses or individuals that harbor prejudices against certain consumers.

Laws protect rights

The overall purpose of any consumer law is to protect the three basic rights of the consumer, which includes the right to safety, the right to be informed, and the right to be treated fairly. Federal and state laws are usually designed around protecting one or more of these basic rights and may include protections against products that are outright dangerous, protections against deceptive business tactics or hidden costs associated with a transaction, and protections against certain types of

discrimination within the marketplace. Even though these rights may not be guaranteed in all situations, there are both federal and state laws intended to protect the consumer's safety, inform the consumer as much as possible regarding products, services, and the costs associated with those products, and prevent unfair discrimination whenever possible. Ultimately, these state and federal laws are designed to hold businesses accountable for the manner in which they conduct business.

ECOA and Fair Housing Act

The Equal Credit Opportunity Act (ECOA) is a federal act that prohibits any organization that issues credit to consumers from denying a consumer credit on the basis of race, gender, age, marital status, religion, national origin, skin color, and whether or not the consumer is receiving federal aid. The act also prohibits any organization from denying a consumer credit because that consumer has previously used another of their rights granted to them by federal law as long as the consumer used that right without malicious intent. If a consumer is denied credit, the organization issuing the denial is required by law to send the denial notification in writing and the consumer has 60 days to request that the organization send the reason for the denial in writing as well.

The Fair Housing Act (FHA) is a similar anti-discrimination act that prevents a seller or organization offering financing for a home from denying to sell, rent, or finance the home on the basis of race, color, gender, religion, family status, national origin, and handicap.

Fair Credit Reporting Act

The Fair Credit Reporting Act requires that the agencies that collect and distribute information about consumers for credit related purposes, known as consumer reporting agencies, have to follow certain guidelines on how they maintain and distribute the information they collect. This act requires consumer reporting agencies to follow a series of procedures set by law to verify and correct mistakes on a consumer's credit record if the consumer makes a dispute and keep records confidential only releasing them to businesses that have a legitimate need for those records. This act also sets limits to how long certain negative information can be kept on record and if a negative piece of information is removed through a dispute, that information cannot be put back into a consumer's record without notifying the consumer in writing within 5 days. This act was later amended by the Fair and Accurate Credit Transactions Act to allow consumers to receive one free copy of their credit report from the three major consumer reporting agencies each year as well.

Fair Debt Collection Practices Act

The Fair Debt Collection Practices Act requires businesses known as third party debt collectors that collect debts that are not directly due to them, but are rather due to another individual or business to refrain from the use of certain abusive or deceptive practices in collecting those debts. This act prohibits such practices as calling consumers at times other than in between 8:00 a.m. and 9:00 p.m. local time and contacting consumers in any fashion other than filing a lawsuit if the consumer has given written notice not to contact him or her regarding the debt. This act also prohibits the collection agency from such practices as adding extra fees and charges to the original balance unless allowed by law, threatening consumers with arrest or legal action that is not actually possible, or reporting false information on a consumer's credit report. This act also requires third party debt collectors to identify themselves as a debt collector to the consumer during every communication and upon request provide verification of the original debt.

Truth in Lending Act

The Truth in Lending Act requires any organization issuing credit to a consumer to disclose the full terms of the lending arrangement and all costs associated with entering that arrangement. This means that when a consumer applies for a loan, a credit card, or any other type of credit, the organization needs to provide the consumer with information about the finance charge, the annual percentage rate for the loan, and any additional fees for beginning the arrangement. This act also limits the amount of money that a consumer can be held liable for if his or her credit card is lost or stolen and sets a procedure for the fair and timely handling of billing disputes related to credit transactions.

Responsible consumers

Even though there are state and federal laws protecting consumers from unethical business practices, it is not always possible to prevent every type of unscrupulous tactic from being used and consumers therefore need to be careful to avoid being scammed. Many businesses attempt to strictly adhere to societal and legal standards and avoid the use of tactics that are outright illegal or unethical. However, there are still businesses that sometimes choose what is profitable over what is ethical and may find loopholes in regulations, ways of suggesting something that is not necessarily true about their product without committing a crime, and new ways of adding on additional fees. Consumers, in spite of the number of laws designed to protect them, need to be careful to protect their own interests when making transactions in the marketplace.

Caveat emptor

The Latin phrase "caveat emptor" literally means "let the buyer beware." This expression suggests that the buyer needs to beware of products or services that may be outright defective or not as useful as the buyer had intended. Some states have laws that create implied warranties regarding certain types of products that allow the consumer to return a product that is defective. However, even in states that do have implied warranties, it does not protect the consumer from certain kinds of defects and only protects the consumer from defects that show up before a certain period of time has passed. If the product or service is not what the consumer thought it was, but the seller made no deliberate attempt to defraud the consumer, the seller in almost every case is actually under no legal obligation to take the product back and return the consumer's money.

Well-informed consumers

A consumer, before making any purchase that requires the investment of a large amount of resources, needs to gather as much information about the product or service he or she is about to buy. By finding out what other consumers have said about a particular product and discovering exactly what the product is capable of doing and what it is not capable of doing, the consumer can avoid purchasing a product that is defective or less useful than the consumer thought previously. The consumer can also research what kinds of problems other consumers have had with the product in the past and compare the quality and uses of various similar products to see if the product is the best fit for the needs of the consumer. The seller of a particular product is never under any obligation to actually inform the consumer of how the product compares in price, quality, and usefulness to other products and the consumer needs to be aware of what he or she is actually purchasing.

Wants versus needs

A want is anything that a person desires while a need is anything that a person actually requires to continue functioning. For example, someone may want a brand new big screen TV, but the television is not actually necessary to an individual's continued survival so this is something that the individual wants, but does not need. An example of a need, on the other hand, might be food and water, which is actually something that the individual requires to survive. Each individual has his or her own wants or desires, but needs are more universal as they are the basic necessities that each individual needs to satisfy. However, no individual is usually ever able to fulfill all of his or her wants because a person usually has more desires than his or her resources can fulfill.

Consumer decision process

The first step of the decision process for any consumer is actually recognizing that the consumer has a need or a want that he or she wishes to fulfill. After the want or need has been established, the consumer will usually attempt to gather information about products or services that will fulfill that need or want by searching online,

- 32 -

searching magazines and advertisements, or talking with other people. The consumer will then evaluate the various products or services to determine which option will best fulfill that need or want. Once the consumer's options have been evaluated, the consumer will actually decide which product or service to purchase and make the purchase. Finally, after the purchase is complete, the consumer will decide whether or not that product or service really satisfied the initial want or need that began the process in the first place.

Marketing

Marketing is the process of informing as many consumers as possible of the existence of a particular seller's product or service and the benefits of that product or service for the purpose of influencing the consumer's purchasing decisions. In other words, marketing is a combination of tactics, including many different forms of advertising, which individuals, businesses, and other organizations use to convince consumers to purchase their products. Marketing is important because it allows businesses to play a large role in what consumers actually purchase. Consumers may have the final say in what products or services they actually decide to use, but marketing can make certain products seem more apparent, more useful, and of a higher quality than a consumer would normally believe them to be. Marketing can also sometimes be useful to consumers by informing them about various useful products within the marketplace, however, consumers still need to be wary of claims and advertisements made by marketers that may make products seem better than they really are.

Marketing can influence almost every stage of the consumer's purchase decision process, but it has the greatest direct effect on the first three stages. The first stage of the process can actually be triggered through an advertisement that is marketing a particular product that the consumer would not normally think of as necessary. A business, by creating the image that a product or service is something necessary to the consumer, can make something the consumer wants appear to be something the consumer needs. Marketing can also directly influence the second and third stages of the decision making process by making it appear that a particular product is better or more useful than competing products even though this may not necessarily be the case. The marketing process can even indirectly influence the fourth stage of the process, where a consumer actually purchases the product, because the consumer has the preconceived notion that a certain product is better than other similar products as a result of the advertisements that they have seen.

State of the economy

The economy plays a large role in how careful consumers are when using their resources and ultimately what they allow themselves to perceive as needs and what they perceive as wants. When the economy is doing well, and there is no shortage of jobs and a lower risk of consumers being unable to procure the basic necessities they require, consumers will usually be more willing to spend their financial resources. Consumers will also be more willing to spend their resources on products and services that are not necessary to their survival, but are instead products and services that the consumer simply enjoys having and may increase his or her quality of living. However, when the economy as a whole is not doing well, there is a shortage of jobs, and a significantly higher risk of consumers being unable to acquire basic necessities due to a lack of income, consumers are much more likely to cut back on their spending.

Environmental concerns

The condition of the natural environment can have a large effect on the purchasing decisions of a consumer in two major ways. First, most consumers are at least somewhat concerned with the state of the environment around them, due to their own personal values or societal values, and therefore will often seek ways to prevent unnecessary waste. Virtually no one will always purchase the most environmental-friendly products and conserve every possible resource at all times, but consumers will often choose to purchase products that are recycled or less wasteful when they are available and those products are not significantly more expensive. The second major way that the environment can affect the purchasing decisions of a consumer is when a consumer decides to conserve a particular resource because that resource becomes more expensive due to a shortage. For example, if there is a gas shortage in a particular area, the prices of gas will rise significantly, and consumers will often attempt to conserve gas to avoid paying higher prices.

The primary way that consumers can help protect the environment is by conserving natural resources and finding ways to reduce pollution and waste. Some of the best ways to conserve natural resources are by reducing the amount of resources that a household uses, finding ways of using resources in a more efficient fashion, and reusing resources rather than simply discarding them. For example, a household can reduce the amount of resources it uses by making sure the lights and heat are off in an unused room or make heating a room more efficient by insulating outside walls to reduce the amount of heat that is wasted. A household can also reuse resources either through recycling or simply using a cardboard box that a product came in to store other household items.

Environmental economics

Environmental economics is the study of the effects that businesses or consumers can have on the overall financial and natural environment when operating within set limits. Basically, what this means is that environmental economics ultimately studies how much pollution actually costs based on the financial costs or savings associated with pollution and the amount of environmental resources lost due to that pollution. Environmental economics is important to businesses and consumers as it can influence what products are available and what processes can be used in manufacturing those products. This influence is a result of the laws and regulations that are made, based on environmental economists' recommendations, to reduce the amount of damage done to the financial and natural environment due to the inefficient use of natural resources. Even though these laws are ultimately to prevent natural resources from being wasted, these regulations often lead to certain products being eliminated from the marketplace or significant cost increases to the end consumers as businesses incur additional costs in meeting those regulations.

Consumer agencies

There are countless agencies that can provide resources that help inform consumers of the advantages, disadvantages, and even the scams

- 34 -

related to certain products and services. Some of the government agencies that are most useful to consumers are the Federal Citizen Information Center, the Consumer Product Safety Commission, the National Fraud Information Center, and the Federal Trade Commission. All of these agencies have extensive information online as well as print publications available about most of the common products on the market. Probably the most well known and useful private agencies to consumers are Consumer's Research, which is a non-profit agency that publishes the magazine Consumer Reports, and the Better Business Bureau, which is a private organization made up of businesses that sets certain standards that its members are expected to follow.

Health care services

A consumer that is in need of health care services may want to consider the number of complaints and the type of complaints a facility or specific doctor has received and examine the qualifications of the doctors who practice in that facility. These factors are important to the consumer for any health care decision ranging from choosing a physician for a simple examination to choosing a surgeon for a complex surgery as they give the consumer a basic idea of the quality and reliability of the overall medical facility. By determining the number of complaints and the types of complaints that have been filed against a particular doctor or facility, a consumer can get an idea of what kinds of mistakes and how many of those mistakes the facility or doctor has made. Experience can also be a key factor in how reliable a particular doctor is and greatly effect the quality of his or her care as usually more experienced doctors will be capable of providing more effective care.

Unfortunately, it can often be difficult to determine exactly how many complaints a particular physician or facility has had filed against them as there is no federal law requiring physicians of facilities to disclose or even report information regarding complaints. However, the United States Department of Health and Services does keep track of reported complaints and is a good place to start for a consumer that is attempting to gather information about a particular doctor or medical facility. Certain states also have laws that do require medical facilities to report the number of complaints and the nature of those complaints filed against the facility or specific doctors employed by the facility. In many of these states, the facility may not be obligated to directly disclose the information to patients, but a consumer can usually access a state database containing the information online.

Child care services

There are a lot of factors that a consumer may want to consider when attempting to decide which child care service to use. Some of the most important factors are how many children each teacher or caregiver has to take care of, what qualifications do the teachers or caregivers have, how long those teachers or caregivers worked for the facility have, and is the facility appropriately licensed and accredited. The number of children that a particular caregiver needs to care for at one time as well as how many children there are overall in the facility at one time can have a large role in how much time each caregiver has for each child. It is also important that a consumer makes sure that not only the facility itself is accredited and licensed, but that the teachers or caregivers that actually work with the children have the knowledge and experience necessary to care for them.

There are many resources available to consumers who are attempting to find the best child care available in their area, but one of the best sources of information is usually the child care facilities themselves. A consumer, by visiting the child care centers that they are interested in, can actually gather most of the information the consumer needs about a particular facility first hand such as how many children does the facility take care of at one time. A consumer can also usually find information regarding the facility's accreditation while visiting the facility as well, but it is always a good idea to verify that the accreditation is valid and accurate. The Child Care Bureau, which is a subdivision of the United States Department of Health and Human Services, has services available to help consumers locate local organizations that will verify the accreditation of a child care provider. The Child Care Bureau can also be a useful resource for finding additional information about local child care programs.

Elder care services

The first step of the process of choosing a facility to care for an elderly family member is realizing that the family member needs assistance beyond what the rest of the family could normally offer. After the family realizes that the elderly individual needs additional care, the second step is to evaluate the needs of the family member. The consumer, by having a basic idea of what the elderly individual is capable of doing on his or her own and what they need assistance for, will be able to seek out facilities that better suit the needs of the individual. The next step of the process that the family should perform is gathering information regarding facilities in the area that fit the needs of the elderly individual. Finally,

the family should actually choose the facility that appears to best suit those needs.

It is important to know the needs of an elderly person and find the elder care facility that best suits those needs because each elderly individual functions at a different level of ability. As each individual has different capabilities and needs, there is also a difference between how well each facility is able to take care of the different needs of each patient. It is also important to make sure that the elderly individual is placed in the environment that allows them the most freedom and is the closest match to their current level of functioning. For example, it is not necessary to place a woman that is capable of performing normal activities such as bathing, eating, and moving around on her own in a nursing home. However, if the woman is at higher risk of injuring herself due to medical conditions associated with old age and there often is no one available to assist the woman, a panic button or an assisted living home may be appropriate options.

A consumer that is attempting to decide upon the appropriate elder care facility for an elderly family member may want to start by using resources available from the Administration on Aging. The Administration on Aging is a division of the Department of Health and Human Services that offers resources for locating local care facilities as well as state and local agencies that monitor those facilities so the consumer can get a better idea of what kinds of facilities are available. Another resource that is available to the consumer is the National Institute of Aging, which provides consumers with a variety of publications regarding the needs and health concerns of elderly individuals as well as an online database for finding local care facilities. Regardless of which resources a consumer chooses to use, the best resource is often going to visit the facilities in person to see what kind of services they can offer and what problems the facility has overall.

Repair services

A consumer that is attempting to find a particular type of repair service in the nearby area can often find additional information about local repair shops, garages, etc. from the local Better Business Bureau. Each Better Business Bureau consists of a number of area businesses that are expected to uphold a certain standard of operation and in return the Better Business Bureau helps suggest member businesses in good standing to consumers. If the consumer is considering using a repair service that belongs to a larger chain of stores, it is often a good idea to check publications such as Consumer Reports to see if there have been problems or complaints against the chain in the past. Even if these publications make the chain look like a good option, the consumer may still want to check with the local Better Business Bureau as each store within a chain can often have their own problems and complaints that are separate from the chain itself.

Safety resources

The best resources that a consumer can use when attempting to determine if a product is safe for the consumer's child or family are Consumer Reports, the Consumer Product Safety Commission, and the National Fraud Information Center. Consumer Reports offers a variety of reviews and information regarding the quality of most common products as well as common defects and complaints that consumers have reported with those products. The Consumer Product Safety Commission offers consumers access to a number of publications regarding what to look for when spotting dangerous products as well as listings of products that have already been recalled or shown to have potentially dangerous defects. The National Fraud Information Center can also be an important resource as they offer consumers information about products that businesses may have deliberately hidden or outright lied about in an attempt to make their products more appealing to consumers.

Family budget

A family that has decided to create a family budget should start by determining how much money the family has on hand and how much income the family receives annually. Next, the family should determine what expenses the family has to pay and which of those expenses are necessary and which expenses are luxuries. Necessary expenses might include housing, food, utilities, child care, health care, transportation, insurance, etc. Luxuries might include eating at restaurants, going to the movies, buying a bigger TV, and other activities that are not necessary to the family's continued survival. The third step that a family should take when making a budget is adding up all of the total necessary expenses and subtracting the total from the family's total annual income. This gives the family the total annual income after necessary expenses, which the family should then decide how much of that money would go into the family's savings. The remaining money can then be budgeted for other less necessary activities that the family wishes to perform.

Credit

Credit is the ability of a consumer to purchase a product or service now and pay for that product in full or in installments at a later time. Credit can be extremely useful to a consumer or an entire family as it offers a way of handling larger expenses, such as purchasing a house, when the consumer or family does not have enough funds on hand to make the purchase. However, it is important that an individual or family as a whole remembers that purchases made using credit need to be paid back and keeping track of their credit and the purchases that they make using it is extremely important. If a consumer fails to pay back the bank or credit card company that loaned them the money for the purchase, or even just fails to pay an installment on time, it can greatly impact the ability of the consumer to get credit in the future.

Some tactics that might be useful to a consumer attempting to manage their credit more carefully are making sure to pay bills on time, avoiding purchases that the family or consumer cannot afford, keeping track of how much debt the family or consumer has, and monitoring the family's credit report. A consumer or family that avoids making purchases that they can't afford are much more likely to be able to pay back the loans that they take out on time, which will help keep the consumer's credit in good standing. If the consumer or family avoids making too many purchases or taking out too many loans, it will also be easier for the consumer to pay back those loans and extensive debt can negatively influence an individual's credit. Closely monitoring the consumer's credit report is also important as it gives the consumer a chance to dispute claims that may be negatively influencing his or her credit, but were placed on the credit report by mistake.

Investments

Investment is the process of committing an individual or family's resources to a particular activity, organization, or fund, with the hope that that commitment will provide additional resources for the individual or family in the future. It is important for an individual to make investments and begin saving for retirement as early as possible because it may be more difficult for an individual to maintain their status of living if they do not have sufficient funds set aside when he or she retires. Living expenses increase yearly and even individuals that have set aside money may have difficulty supporting themselves when they start to get older and are less capable of working on a daily basis. Individuals who do not have enough money set aside when they retire may also put additional strain on other family members as they may need the family to help support them financially. However, through careful investment planning, an individual can make sure that his or her financial resources are growing as much as possible.

Some of the factors that an individual or family might want to consider when making investment decisions are the risk of the investment, the potential return of the investment, and how difficult it is to cash-out the investment. The risk of the investment refers simply to how likely it is that the individual or family will gain some benefit from the investment and how likely it is that the individual or family will lose the resources that they have invested. The potential return of the investment refers to how much money is the individual or family likely to earn from the investment through cashing-out the investment or from interest or dividends over time. The amount of difficulty to cash-out the investment is an

- 38 -

important factor because different investments have different costs, taxes, lengths of time to mature, and lengths of time it takes to access the money associated with them.

Investments such as checking accounts, savings accounts, and CDs are usually virtually no risk investments, but they also offer a lower return. These investments are incredibly safe because the bank guarantees that these accounts will earn a certain amount of interest, but the rate of interest is usually relatively low. CDs usually offer somewhat higher rates of interest, but they are more difficult to liquidate as they usually have a set length of time to mature and often can only be liquidated at certain times set by the bank. Mutual funds are usually a low to mid risk investment as there is the potential for the individual or family to lose the resources that they invested, but there is also a higher potential return. Mutual funds are a relatively safe investment as the stock portfolios that the funds go towards are usually heavily diversified and have a lot of different types of stocks that are relatively stable, but they usually have a lower potential return than other higher risk stocks.

A family that is attempting to plan out which investments to make should first consider what are the financial needs that the family hopes to satisfy from these investments. For example, if the family is investing their resources to send their children to college, the family should attempt to determine how much money they will need to pay for college in the future. After the family has determined how much money they need, they can begin researching to determine which investments are likely to offer enough financial gains to reach their financial goals. Once the family has identified which investments might meet their

goals, they should assess how much risk each investment carries and ultimately how likely it is that they might lose money on the investment. Finally, the family should choose the investment that has the lowest risk while still meeting their financial goals.

Retirement

An individual that is attempting to plan how much money he or she needs to invest or put aside for retirement should start by examining how much the individual spends on living expenses and add up all of those expenses with the exception of health care. Once the individual has totaled up all of his or her monthly expenses except for health care, he or she should multiply that number by 1.5 and multiply the health care expenses by 2 to determine how much those expenses will increase in ten years. The individual then needs to estimate how many years it will be until the individual retires and for each additional ten years multiply the health care expenses by 2 and all other expenses by 1.5 again. Finally, by adding these two results together, the individual will have the total estimated monthly expenses adjusted for inflation. This gives the individual a rough estimate of how much they will need for each month after they retire.

Insurance

The major types of insurance that an individual or family might need are health insurance, homeowner's insurance, life insurance, and car insurance. The reason that a family should have these types of insurance is that a problem in any of these areas can have a significant impact on the financial security of the individual or family as a whole. Health problems, fire, theft, the death of a provider in the family, or a car accident can all lead to additional expenses that the individual or family may not be able to afford. Having these types of insurance offers individuals and families a way of paying the unexpected expenses associated with handling these problems without significantly impacting the overall financial well-being of the individual or family.

Checking and savings accounts

Some of the things that an individual or family should consider when attempting to open a checking or saving account are what are the minimum balance requirements, what fees are there for having the account, and what is the annual interest earned by the account. Most banks charge account holders for having less than the minimum balance required in their account and often have additional fees for ATM use and other services that can make the account more expensive to the consumer than an individual might realize. If the financial institution is charging a significant number of fees, but is not offering a high interest rate on the account, it may be a good idea for the consumer to seek out another institution. It is also very important that the individual or family makes sure that the bank, credit unions, or any other institution that they are considering placing money into is insured by the federal government through the Federal Deposit Insurance Corporation (FDIC) or the National Credit Union Administration (NCUA.)

Product labels

Product labels are important because they act as a way of marking various products with information that can be useful or even vital to consumers. A label is nothing more than a tag that is attached to a product, but it can inform a consumer

about the ingredients of the product, the materials used in the construction of the product, the appropriate manner to use the product, or hazards caused by using the product incorrectly. This information can be useful for determining which products suit the needs of the consumer, but are also safe for the consumer to use around children and other family members. For example, a label would allow a consumer to determine whether or not a particular piece of clothing is made out of a strong enough material for the use that the consumer had intended and that the material is something the consumer is not allergic to.

Warranties

A warranty, also known as a guarantee, is a promise made by the seller of a particular product or service that that product or service will function as advertised or the seller will attempt to repair or replace the product or perform the service again. Warranties usually only apply if the product or service fails to function when the consumer is using the product correctly and there are often many other conditions that must be met for the seller to carry out the terms of the warranty. For example, most warranties only require that the seller replace or repair a product if that product fails within a certain length of time. Warranties are important to consumers because they offer a certain amount of protection against purchasing products that fail immediately or shortly after leaving the store. However, many warranties also place limits on what types of repairs the seller is required to perform so consumers need to be aware of the terms and conditions of a warranty before making a purchase.

Consumer advocacy groups

- 40 -

Consumer advocacy groups, such as the Consumer's Union, the Better Business Bureau, the Consumer Federation of America, the Center for Science in the Public Interest, and Consumer Alert are all organizations that attempt to protect consumers from unsafe products and unethical business practices. Many of these groups often conduct research on various products and offer the results of their research to consumers either online or through their publications to warn consumers of safety concerns, defects, or scams associated with certain products or services. Consumer advocacy groups also organize and fund campaigns targeted at encouraging support for legislation that promotes fair and ethical business practices as well as legislation that ultimately protects the rights of consumers. Consumer advocacy groups are not only a good source of information to consumers that are attempting to make a decision about which product or service to use, but are also an important ally to consumers who have had problems with a particular product or service and need assistance.

Nutrition and Food

Nutritional needs

Some of the major factors that can affect an individual's nutritional needs are the age of the individual, the individual's gender, and his or her level of activity. The age of the individual plays a major role in the nutritional needs that a particular person has because as a child grows, the number of calories the child needs also grows, but after the individual passes a certain age the number of calories the individual needs then decreases. The individual's need for specific vitamins and minerals also increases as the individual becomes older. Gender can affect an individual's nutritional needs because men typically require more protein and more calories than women do and women usually require significantly more iron than men require. The individual's level of activity also plays a large role in his or her nutritional needs as an individual that is more active will require a larger amount of calories than an individual who less active.

Activity level

A low activity individual is usually considered to be any individual that does not regularly exercise and gets less than 30 minutes of exercise on any given day. A high activity individual is usually considered to be any individual that regularly exercises and gets at least 30 to 60 minutes of exercise 4 to 5 times a week. An individual can also be considered high activity if they are in a profession that is physically intense such as warehouse workers, moving company workers, gym teachers, etc... Individuals that exercise more than 30 minutes at a time, but do so only once or twice a week are usually considered mid-level activity individuals rather than high or low activity individuals.

Needs of less active

The nutritional needs of an individual change in a variety of different ways as the individual ages, but the major changes involve which vitamins the body requires and the number of calories that the individual requires to keep functioning. Young children usually only require around 1000 to 1500 calories a day, but the amount of calories a child requires increases as the child grows. Young teens usually require somewhere between 1600 and 2200 calories a day, depending on their gender and other factors. Individuals entering young adulthood usually require between 2000 and 2400 calories a day. However, after the individual reaches age 30, the amount of calories the individual needs begins to decrease as they get older. Each individual will also require progressively more Vitamins A, C, and E as well as iron and fiber as they age. Individuals over age 50 also require significantly more calcium.

Needs of highly active

An individual that is more active requires more calories than an individual who is less active. A young active child usually requires around the same number of calories as a less active child, but the difference between the calorie needs of an individual that is less active and an individual that is more active increases substantially as the child grows. Active young teens require 1600 to 2600 calories, depending on gender and other factors and active individuals entering young adulthood usually require between 2000 and 3200 calories. As these age

- 42 -

ranges show, the calorie needs of an active individual is usually between 400 – 800 calories higher than a less active individual. Active individuals also require more protein than less active individuals, but usually require similar amounts of Vitamins A, C, and E as well as iron and fiber.

Calcium

Calcium is important to the development and maintenance of an individual's bones and teeth as a lack of calcium can result in osteoporosis and other bone problems. Calcium is also important to the body's production of lymph, which is a fluid similar to interstitial fluid that aids in the overall operation of the individual's body specifically in regards to the immune system. Common sources that an individual might use to get more calcium are milk, cheese, honey, egg, orange juice, oranges, broccoli, rutabagas, almonds and other nuts. Calcium can also be obtained through supplements and multivitamins, which can be a good source to individuals that are allergic to dairy products or have a significant calcium deficiency. Both men and women require similar amounts of calcium, but the amount of calcium that an individual requires increases as the individual ages.

Iron

Iron is important because it aids in the proper functioning of virtually all of the individual's muscles and organs. Iron also allows the body to form hemoglobin, which is a protein that is found in red blood cells that carries oxygen throughout the body. If an individual does not have enough iron in his or her diet, this can result in a condition known as anemia where the body is unable to produce hemoglobin. The body may also be unable to produce additional red blood cells if there is a lack of iron in the individual's system and the individual will be more likely to become fatigued and develop other symptoms and conditions as well. Common sources of iron that an individual might use include oatmeal, spaghetti, whole wheat bread, sunflower seeds, broccoli, green beans, beats, peas, potatoes, other green leafy vegetables, beef, pork, and chicken. Women usually require more iron than men do partially due to the regular blood loss associated with menstruation.

Vitamin A

Vitamin A, also known as retinol, is important because it aids in an individual's bone growth, skin health, and ability to reproduce. Vitamin A also promotes eye health and aids in the production of tears to prevent each eye from drying out as well as washing away bacteria that might cause infections. A vitamin A deficiency can cause the eyes to deteriorate and may lead to conditions such as night blindness, also known as nyctalopia, where an individual has difficulty seeing in low light environments. Common sources of vitamin A include carrots, sweet potatoes, pumpkins, spinach, beef, pork, chicken, eggs, and broccoli. Both men and women require similar amounts of vitamin A for their bodies to function normally, but men usually require slightly more than women do.

Vitamin C

Vitamin C, also known as ascorbic acid, is important because it helps protect the health of the individual's skin, bones, teeth, cartilage, and blood vessels. Vitamin C protects these areas of the body primarily by acting as an antioxidant that helps reduce the negative effects that oxygen reactions within the body can

- 43 -

have on the body's cells. Vitamin C is also necessary in the production of collagen, which is a protein necessary for skin and cartilage health. Significant vitamin C deficiencies can result in a number of serious health problems including a disorder known as scurvy where the body lacks the collagen it requires to maintain the health of the skin ultimately leading to the formation of liver spots on the individual's skin and gums. Scurvy can also cause an individual to bleed from all of the body's mucous membranes including the nose, lips, and ears as well as other areas. Common sources of vitamin C include strawberries, oranges, lemons, limes, mangos, grapes, broccoli, potatoes, spinach, liver, and milk.

Vitamin E

Vitamin E, also known as tocopherol, is important primarily because it aids in maintaining proper brain function and eye health. It has also been suggested that vitamin E may help reduce an individual's risk of cancer, cataracts, heart disease, and other health conditions as well as helping treat patients that have Parkinson's or Alzheimer's Disease. A significant vitamin E deficiency can result in muscle weakness, blindness, and neurological problems as a result of the body transmitting nerve impulses incorrectly. Common sources of vitamin E include peanuts, hazelnuts, coconuts, corn, asparagus, carrots, tomatoes, fish, peanut butter, and vegetable oils. There are also many multivitamins and supplements that supply vitamin E, but some studies have shown that some synthetic vitamins and supplements may actually be significantly less beneficial or even have a negative impact on the individual when taken in large doses. However, both men and women do require vitamin E, in similar amounts, to continue functioning normally.

Fiber

Fiber is an important part of an individual's diet because it helps with the body's bowel movements, digestion, and immune responses. Fiber has also been shown to lower blood cholesterol, help prevent obesity, lower the risk of certain types of cancer including specifically colon cancer, and lower the risk of type 2 diabetes. A significant lack of fiber in an individual's diet can lead to symptoms such as constipation and slower digestion and can cause an individual to have a higher risk of developing certain diseases. Some common sources of fiber include certain breakfast cereals, oatmeal, whole-wheat bread, beans, apples, pears, strawberries, bananas, potatoes, onions, and green beans. Both men and women require similar amounts of fiber to continue functioning properly.

Vitamin B12

B12, also known as cyanocobalamin, is important because it is necessary for the production of blood cells and it aids in maintaining the health of the nervous system. A severe lack of B12 within the body can lead to a variety of conditions including megaloblastic anemia, which is a condition where the red blood cells have less hemoglobin and therefore will have more difficulty functioning properly. A significant lack of B12 can also lead to severe problems with the individual's nervous system mainly due to the lack of B12 causing the disintegration of the nerve cells and eventually the death of those cells. Individuals who lack significant quantities of B12 may develop symptoms such as numbness, tingling, and difficulty with muscle control. Some common sources of B12 include chicken, beef, pork, liver, fish, shellfish, certain breakfast cereals, milk, cheese, eggs, and

- 44 -

yogurt. Vegetarians may have difficulty getting enough B12 as the primary sources of B12 are meat products, but B12 supplements and multivitamins can be a good option as well.

Protein

Protein is important to the functioning of a healthy individual because protein is necessary for the body to produce the amino acids it needs to continue functioning. Most of the amino acids that the body needs to function are already present in the body, but certain amino acids, known as essential amino acids, can only be produced when the body digests protein breaking it down into smaller components. A severe lack of protein is usually caused by malnutrition and can lead to reduced brain function, mental retardation, and an overall weakening of the immune system due to a decrease in the number of white blood cells. It has also been suggested that a significant lack of protein may lead to certain conditions such as kwashiokor, which causes significant weight loss, thinning and discolored hair, swelling of the organs, and weakens the responses of the individual's immune system. Some common sources of protein include chicken, beef, wheat, rice, milk, cheese, eggs, peas, beans, peanuts, and peanut butter.

RDA versus RDI

RDA stands for recommended dietary allowance, which is the amount of each vitamin, mineral, or other nutrient that health professionals believe an individual needs to receive daily in order to stay healthy. The RDA has been replaced by the now more commonly used RDI or reference daily intake. The RDI is similar to the RDA, but does not recommend different nutrient intakes based on

gender and age as the RDA does. The RDI is used to determine the RDV, or recommended daily value, which is printed on virtually every food product in the United States and Canada to inform consumers of the nutritional value, or the lack thereof, that each product offers. These recommended daily values are usually based on a 2000-calorie diet and since the RDI recommends the same nutrient intake for everyone, there is no difference shown between the intakes necessary for individuals of different age groups or genders. Both the RDA and RDI are important because they allow consumers to determine which foods are best for their diet.

Dietary Guidelines for Americans

The Dietary Guidelines for Americans is a combined publication of the United States Department of Health and Human Services and the United States Department of Agriculture that offers advice to consumers about dietary choices that promote good health and reduce the risk of certain diseases including hypertension, anemia, and osteoporosis. The Dietary Guidelines for Americans offers advice to consumers on a variety of topics such as weight management, appropriate exercise, food safety, and examples of good sources of certain nutrients. This publication is important because it offers a detailed outline of the kinds of foods that an individual should have in their diets so they do not need to use additional supplements and vitamins. It also informs consumers of the types of exercise that are necessary for an individual to stay healthy as well as the appropriate manner in which to handle and prepare certain foods to minimize the risk of foodborne illness.

USDA Daily Food Guide

- 45 -

The United States Department of Agriculture's Daily Food Guide, also known as the food pyramid, is a diagram that splits the dietary needs of a healthy individual into a series of food groups that the individual needs to eat a certain amount from each group daily to stay healthy. These groups include grains, vegetables, fruits, oils, milk, and meat and beans, which are organized into a color-coded pyramid. Exactly how much of each category an individual needs to consume to stay healthy depends largely on the individual's age, gender, and weight, but the pyramid offers a basic set of guidelines for consumption that can be used regardless of these factors. Some of the basic guidelines the pyramid sets are that individuals should eat at least 3 ounces of whole grain products a day, eat more dark green and orange vegetables as well as peas and beans, and eat a variety of fruits, but avoid fruit juices.

Anorexia

Anorexia is an eating disorder where an individual views his or her own body as being overweight, even though he or she is not, causing the individual to have an extreme, unfounded fear of gaining additional weight. This fear can lead individuals to use desperate and unhealthy methods to reduce their weight below what would normally be healthy including deliberate vomiting, limiting their food intake, exercising excessively without eating enough food, or by using medications to flush their system. Anorexia is commonly found to affect young women, specifically during adolescence and the teenage years, and can pose a serious risk to an individual's health as the obsessive attempts to reduce the individual's body weight can affect the health of the individual's heart, brain, immune system, muscles, and other organs. Anorexia can be extremely difficult to treat as it is a complicated psychological condition, but it has been shown that psychotherapy may be able to help the individual overcome the inaccurate perceptions that the individual has regarding his or her own body.

Bulimia

Bulimia is an eating disorder, similar to anorexia, where an individual views his or her own body as being unattractive or overweight, but lacks the ability to control his or her own eating. Bulimic individuals regularly eat an unhealthily large amount of food and then attempt to flush their systems to prevent themselves from gaining additional weight due to the large amounts of food that the individual consumed. Some of the methods individuals suffering from bulimia might use to flush food from their systems include deliberate vomiting, excessive exercise, or using diet pills, laxatives, ipecac, and other medications. Bulimia is most commonly found in women, especially younger women from ages 12 to 19, and can have a significant impact on the health of the individual causing problems such as anemia, weakness, muscle and heart problems, dehydration, malnutrition, damage to the stomach, and a wide range of other problems. Bulimia is difficult to treat, but a combination of group psychotherapy and low doses of anti-psychotics have been shown to help.

Anorexia versus bulimia

Anorexia and bulimia are very similar disorders, but there is one major difference between the two conditions and that difference is control. An individual suffering from anorexia is usually already below a healthy weight and still perceives that his or her own weight is unacceptable and therefore he

- 46 -

or she attempts to lower that weight further below what would normally be healthy by controlling his or her own food intake. Bulimic individuals, on the other hand, have no sense of control over their own eating habits and instead eat excessively and then attempt to overcompensate for their excessive food intake. Individuals suffering from anorexia are usually below what would normally be considered a healthy weight for their age and size and attempt to control their eating to reduce their weight further, bulimic individuals, however, are usually above a healthy weight as they have no control over their own eating.

Obesity

Obesity is a condition of the body where the individual has increased his or her own body weight significantly beyond what is normally considered healthy usually due to excessive eating. Obesity occurs because the individual takes in more food than his or her body can actually use and the excess food is stored as fat. Overeating is the primary cause of obesity, but obesity can also be tied to family history, genetic factors, stress and lack of sleep, various illnesses and conditions, and many other causes. An individual who is obese puts themselves at a significantly higher risk for certain health problems including problems with the heart, stomach, muscles, lungs, skin, nervous system, and many other areas of the body. The best way to treat obesity is through a well balanced diet that eliminates the excessive intake of food beyond what the individual needs along with the use of a rigorous exercise program. In extreme cases, individuals may also use medication or even surgery to help lower their weight.

Preventing eating disorders

Unfortunately, there is no known way of completely eliminating the risk of an individual developing an eating-related condition such as anorexia, bulimia, and obesity, but it has been shown that some methods may significantly lower the risk of individuals developing these conditions. The best way to reduce the risk of an individual developing an eating disorder or becoming obese is for parents to interact more with their children and make sure that they are teaching their children good eating habits early on. It is also important that parents attempt to build-up the self-esteem of their children through interactions that show high esteem in both the parents and child. Children who have been taught good eating habits by their parents and who have been taught to have high self-esteem have been shown to eat more carefully and therefore are at a significantly lower risk of both becoming obese and developing eating disorders like anorexia and bulimia.

Diabetes

Diabetes is a disease that prevents the body from producing and using a hormone called insulin, which the body needs to process sugar and use it as energy for the cells of the body. Since an individual with diabetes cannot produce insulin, the body is unable to appropriately use the sugar that the cells need to survive and the sugar instead builds up in the individual's body leading to a high sugar concentration in the blood, which is a condition known as hyperglycemia. Diabetes can lead to a series of dangerous health problems including the potential failure of the heart, kidneys, nerves, and eyes as well as conditions such as high blood pressure, blindness, poor healing of wounds, and many other dangerous conditions. There is currently no cure for diabetes, but the

- 47 -

negative effects of diabetes can be controlled through careful monitoring of blood sugar levels, the use of a specific diet to maintain the individual's blood sugar, and through the use of certain drugs and/or insulin shots.

The three types of diabetes are type 1, type 2, and gestational diabetes. Type 1 diabetes is a form of diabetes where the individual's own immune system mistakes the beta cells of the pancreas, which are the cells responsible for producing insulin, as being harmful and therefore attacks and destroys them. Type 1 diabetes prevents the individual from actually producing insulin and can be treated primarily through the use of a carefully constructed diet and through insulin injections or the use of an insulin pump. Both type 2 diabetes and gestational diabetes are where the individual is either unable to produce enough insulin for the body or the cells of the body are unable to use the insulin correctly. Type 2 and gestational diabetes can both be treated through the use of a carefully monitored diet along with medication to help the body use the insulin appropriately. The only major difference between type 2 diabetes and gestational diabetes is that gestational diabetes occurs specifically due to hormones present during pregnancy.

There is currently no way to completely prevent an individual from developing diabetes, but the risk of an individual developing certain forms of diabetes can be reduced. The risk of type 2 diabetes and gestational diabetes can be reduced by eating a more healthy diet high in fiber and whole grains, exercising regularly, and lowering the amount of high fat foods that the individual eats. It has also been suggested that the risk of a mother developing gestational diabetes may be reduced through breast-feeding as it

allows the mother to release some of the excess hormones present in her body as a result of the pregnancy. The risk of type 2 and gestational diabetes can be reduced, but there is unfortunately no known way of preventing type 1 diabetes as researchers know very little about the exact causes of the disease.

Hypertension

Hypertension is a condition where an individual's blood pressure is regularly higher than the range that is normally acceptable. The blood pressure of a healthy individual should be somewhere between 90/50 to 120/80 and anything over 140/90 is considered to be a high blood pressure. Anything between 120/80 and 140/90 is considered to be prehypertension where the individual does not yet have dangerously high blood pressure, but is at significant risk of developing hypertension if steps are not taken to lower the individual's blood pressure. Hypertension can significantly impact virtually every part of the body as the increased force of the blood against the individual's artery walls can severely damage the body's organs including the heart, brain, eyes, and kidneys if it goes untreated. Usually there are no apparent symptoms associated with hypertension, but individuals with extremely high blood pressure might experience headaches, vomiting, and difficulty seeing clearly.

Hypertension can usually be treated through the use of a low-salt and low-fat diet along with exercise to bring the individual's blood pressure back down to a reasonable level. People who are being treated for hypertension will usually also be advised to stop smoking and drinking in excess unless it is believed that ceasing these activities will actually put too much additional stress on the individual's body. Individuals with significantly higher

- 48 -

blood pressures will also often be prescribed medication that will help reduce their blood pressure further. There is no way to completely eliminate the risk of hypertension and some factors, including age, race, and family history, can make the individual more predisposed to developing hypertension at some point. However, there are certain factors that individuals can eliminate from their daily activities to significantly lower their risk of developing hypertension. These activities that should be avoided include excessive drinking, smoking, regularly consuming high-salt foods, regular involvement in high-stress activities, and other similar factors that put additional stress on the body.

Cholesterol

Cholesterol is a type of fat known as a lipid that the body uses in the production of new cells and to produce bile, which helps the body digest fat. The body needs a certain amount of cholesterol to continue functioning normally, but excessive amounts of cholesterol can lead to heart and circulatory problems including a condition known as atherosclerosis where the extra cholesterol clogs the arteries. Clogged arteries can cause a variety of other serious problems including heart attacks and strokes as the heart, brain, and many of the other vital organs of the body cannot receive enough blood to function appropriately. One of the best ways to avoid too much cholesterol is to avoid foods that contain high concentrations of saturated fats. Some examples of foods that are high in cholesterol and saturated fats are beef, pork, eggs, milk, butter, cheese, and most snack foods. Some examples of foods that are low in cholesterol and saturated fats include oatmeal, fish, rice, and most fruits and vegetables.

Carbohydrates

Carbohydrates, also known as saccharides, are a group of simple and complex sugars that are primarily important because they supply energy for the body. The body can take these sugars, such as glucose, transport them throughout the body via the bloodstream and break them down into energy that the body can use to keep functioning. Carbohydrates are also important to the effective functioning of the body's immune system, reproductive system, and the body's ability to heal correctly as it helps allow the individual's blood to clot effectively. Many of the functions of carbohydrates can actually be performed from proteins and fats as well, but carbohydrates are easier for the body to digest and contain less cholesterol than proteins and saturated fats. Some examples of foods that are high in carbohydrates include bread, beans, cereals, pasta, potatoes, and rice.

Fats

Fats are important to the healthy functioning of the body as they allow certain vitamins, including vitamins A, D, E, and K, to be digested and absorbed. These fat-soluble vitamins can only be broken down and used by the body when enough fat is present so a lack of certain fats in the individual can lead to other vitamin deficiencies. Fats also help maintain the body's temperature, help promote hair, skin, and overall cell health, protect the body's organs, help protect against some diseases, and act as a means of storing energy for the body to use later. An excess of fat in the body can adversely affect the individual's health, however, as an abundance of saturated fats and trans

- 49 -

fats can greatly increase the cholesterol level in the blood and increase the individual's risk of certain heart conditions and other problems. Some examples of foods that are high in fat and individuals may want to avoid eating in excess include butter, cream, cheese, lard, milk, and snack foods.

Iodine

Relatively small amounts of iodine are important to an individual's health because iodine is necessary for the production of certain hormones, called thyroid hormones, which the body needs to function normally. A severe lack of iodine in an individual's diet or an excessive amount of iodine in the body can lead to a variety of symptoms and conditions including depression, fatigue, mental slowing and retardation, excessive weight gain, and goiter where the individual's neck is extremely swollen. Iodine deficiencies are usually extremely uncommon in the United States and other developed countries because most of the salt used in cooking has been treated with iodine to make sure that individuals take in enough iodine on a daily basis. Some foods that have high iodine contents include iodized salt, fish, kelp, and most dairy products.

Food and beliefs

An individual's religious, moral, and ethical beliefs can play a large part in the individual's diet as certain beliefs can lead to the exclusion of certain foods. Ethical and moral considerations such as preventing animal cruelty or showing disapproval of environmentally unfriendly practices used to acquire certain types of food can lead some individuals to reduce the amount of certain foods they consume, such as meat, or eliminate those foods from their diet completely. For example, many individuals who choose to be vegetarians or vegans usually do so to avoid supporting what they believe to be the unethical slaughter of animals. Religious considerations can also play a large role as certain religions dictate what sort of foods the members of that faith can consume. For example, people practicing Judaism, can only consume kosher foods, which are foods that fit a series of guidelines set by the faith and include restrictions such as how an animal was slaughtered, the type of animal slaughtered, and who prepared the food.

Food and ethnicity

Ethnicity can play an important role in the foods that an individual includes in his or her diet because individuals living in different regions usually have different customs regarding the foods that they eat and different common foods available. For example, individuals living in a country like Japan where there is a large amount of water suitable for fishing will usually consume significantly more fish than individuals living in countries that are landlocked. Individuals who have immigrated to another country or who are descendents of immigrants will also often include foods in their diet that are traditional foods from their native countries even if those foods are not as easily accessible as they would be in their native country. Individuals in certain countries may also include foods in their diets that are not based on how readily available a particular food is, but rather is based on the culture's customary eating habits such as in France where individuals tend to seek out foods that are fresh rather than processed.

Food and satisfaction

- 50 -

Food is extremely important for the health of an individual and can satisfy both some of the basic needs of the individual's body as well as offer some psychological satisfaction as well. Food is a basic necessity to the successful functioning of an individual and therefore the body makes the individual aware of its need for food by making the individual experience a feeling of hunger. When the individual satisfies this hunger by consuming various foods, the body releases hormones that causes the individual to feel a sense of being full and that the hunger is satiated. Certain types of foods sate an individual's hunger more effectively than other foods and foods that are high in fiber, protein, and water usually will make an individual feel more satiated. If an individual's body is lacking a specific type of nutrient, the body will cause the individual to experience a craving for foods that will satisfy that particular need.

Meal planning steps

Individuals or organizations that are attempting to prepare a meal for a group of people where the nutritional value of the meal may be a concern should first decide what the nutritional goals of the meal are. Once these goals have been established, the individual or organization should continue by researching which foods will best satisfy these goals without exceeding their time and resource limits. The individual or organization should then put together a written meal plan that defines exactly which foods will be included, the average time it takes to prepare and cook each of these meals, and the cost associated with preparing these meals. The individual or organization should then attempt to determine the best method of preparing these meals including which foods should be prepared first, the best way to handle or prepare the foods to minimize the risk of illness, and what techniques can be used to reduce the cooking time. Finally, the individual or organization can prepare the meal according to the plan.

Efficiency

Some of the methods that can be used to reduce the time it takes to prepare a meal include keeping the cooking equipment clean and organized, making sure frozen products are thawed beforehand, preparing foods that have long cooking times beforehand, and preparing foods in order of cooking time. By keeping the cooking area and the necessary cooking utensils clean, organized, and easily accessible the individual or organization can make sure that the time they have available is used in the best manner possible. Thawing products beforehand and cooking foods that usually take a long time to cook beforehand and re-heating them later can also greatly reduce the amount of time it takes to prepare the meal when time is a concern. Preparing foods that take a long-time to cook first and then moving onto preparing the foods that take the next longest also greatly reduces preparation time as the individual or organization can prepare other foods in the meal while the foods that take the longest are cooking.

Choosing foods

An individual or organization that is attempting to decide which foods to prepare for a meal should consider the food's nutritional value, the time it takes to prepare each food, the number of people to be served, and the financial cost to prepare each food. Each food has its own distinct cooking times and offers different nutrients so it is important that the individual makes sure to use foods that satisfy their nutritional goals without

- 51 -

violating their time constraints. It is also important that the individual or organization consider the number of people to be served and how much each food costs to prepare as every individual or organization only has a limited amount of resources and certain meals may not be practical for large groups of people. For example, if an individual or organization is attempting to find a good source of protein for a meal, steak might be a good option for a small group of people, but would probably be too expensive for a larger group.

Food types

The two primary types of food that an individual can find in the marketplace are animal products and plant products. Animal products are any foods that are either a piece of an animal or are produced by an animal including foods such as meat, milk, assorted dairy products, honey, etc. Plant products are foods that originate from some sort of vegetation and include foods such as fruits, vegetables, syrup, nuts, oils, rice, etc. It is important for an individual to understand the difference between these two groups as animal products often have different foodborne illness risks associated with them than plant products and therefore there are different methods of storing and preparing each type of food to minimize these risks. Animal products and plant products also often offer different nutrients that the body requires to continue functioning normally so a healthy individual usually needs to eat both animal and plant products to receive enough of the various nutrients they require without the use of supplements.

Available food influences

Some of the major factors that might influence which foods are available to a consumer include the region that the consumer is in, current weather conditions and seasonal effects, and the demand for the particular type of food. Different regions have different natural resources and different climates, which makes different types of foods readily available. For example, certain crops that react poorly to sudden temperature drops such as oranges are easier to grow in areas that have relatively stable and warm climates. Weather and seasonal conditions also have a large effect on whether a particular food is available as certain foods may not be produced during certain times of year in a particular region or may die as a result of hurricanes and other storms. The demand for a particular type of food can also have a significant impact on the availability of that food as well for if the demand for a particular type of food increases suddenly, it may be difficult for suppliers to meet that demand.

Unit pricing

Unit pricing is the practice of indicating the price of a product based on the cost per piece or unit included in that product. In other words, it is a method of determining how much an item costs per unit of measurement. For example, a 12-pack of 12-ounce cans of soda might be $2.99 and have a unit price of $0.70 a liter. Unit pricing is important because it can be extremely useful to a consumer that is attempting to compare two similar products of different sizes to determine which product is the least expensive. For example if an individual is trying to decide between a 12-pack of soda similar to the one in the above example and a six pack that retails for $1.99 and has a unit price of $.93 per liter, the 12 pack is actually the better buy.

Food distributors

- 52 -

Some of the major types of food distributors a consumer might find in the marketplace are chain supermarkets, independent grocery stores and farmers markets, restaurants, and local farm stands. Each type of store has its own distinct advantages and disadvantages. Chain supermarkets are large stores that usually offer a large selection of foods at mid-range prices, but foods are often not as fresh and usually of poorer quality than might be found at a farm stand or farmers market. Independent grocery stores and farmers markets usually have a smaller selection and are slightly more expensive than chain supermarkets, but often purchase food from local sources so the food is more fresh. Restaurants are usually the most expensive distributors of food, but the food is often of a much higher-quality and the food is prepared by the restaurant for the consumer. Local farm stands usually offer the freshest, highest-quality foods for the lowest prices, but are usually only open for shorter periods of time and are not always locally available.

Food consumption patterns

Food consumption patterns are an analysis of the eating habits of people belonging to a particular region or area. Food consumption patterns are important because individuals from different regions have very different diets and therefore receive more of certain nutrients than individuals from other regions might. The kinds of nutrients that are common in the normal diets of individuals native to a particular area are important as they allow individuals and organizations to understand what types of diseases and deficiencies the people of that region might be at a higher risk for. By understanding which diseases and vitamin deficiencies the individuals of a particular area may be suffering, individuals and organizations can focus their resources on treating and preventing those diseases. Monitoring food consumption patterns also allows researchers to study these patterns and determine the ingredients in certain foods that may be contributing to illnesses that are prevalent in a particular region.

Eating preferences

Each individual is fond of certain foods and, at the same time, dislikes or refuses to eat other types of foods. Usually, an individual will find the foods that offer the most physiological and psychological satisfaction as the most appealing. On the other hand, most individuals who refuse to eat a particular food usually refuse to eat that food for one of three basic reasons. These reasons include that the individual dislikes the taste of the food, the condition of the food or how the food was produced disgusts the individual, or the individual fears that the food will make the individual ill. These preferences are important because they are one of the body's safety mechanisms to prevent individuals from eating foods that may be contaminated or that the individual may be allergic to while attempting to consume the nutrients that the body needs. However, these eating preferences may need to be ignored at times so the body can receive all of the nutrients that are necessary.

Government regulations

There are many government regulations that help protect consumers from unsafe foods and help keep the price of various foods down, but some of the most important regulations include food subsidies and price ceilings, tariffs and import quotas, and inspection and sanitation regulations. The government

- 53 -

by imposing tariffs on imported foods, limiting the amount of a particular food that can enter the country, subsidizing farming and food production by offering money to farmers and production facilities, and limiting how much subsidized producers can charge can greatly reduce the price of a particular food. These techniques also ultimately help to keep local food sources in business so the country does not have to rely as much on outside food sources. Government inspection and sanitation regulations such as the Egg Products Inspection Act, the Federal Meat Inspection Act, and the Sanitary Food Transportation Act all help make sure that foods are produced, stored, and transported following certain guidelines to prevent the food from being contaminated.

Reducing foodborne risks

Some of the methods that can be used to reduce the risk of foodborne illness include thawing food appropriately to avoid the risk of bacteria, storing perishable foods in airtight containers and keeping them refrigerated or freezing them, and making sure that all cooking areas and cooking equipment are clean. Individuals should also make sure to wash their hands before and after handling raw foods, wash fruits and vegetables to remove potential bacteria and pesticides, and make sure that foods are cooked at a high enough temperature for a long enough period of time. Perishable foods should be stored in temperatures of 40 degrees Fahrenheit or below to prevent the growth of bacteria and frozen foods should be thawed in the refrigerator rather than at room temperature as bacteria grows most effectively at temperatures between 41 degrees and 140 degrees Fahrenheit. It is also important that meats and other food

products are cooked at a temperature high enough to kill any bacteria that may be present.

Purchasing cooking equipment

Some of the factors that a consumer should consider when attempting to decide which cooking equipment to purchase include the materials used to construct the cooking equipment, the heat conductivity of the materials used, the energy conservation of the cooking equipment, and how easy it is to use the equipment. The materials that are used in the construction of a piece of cooking equipment are extremely important because certain materials conduct heat more effectively, retain heat more efficiently, are more durable, and more inexpensive than other materials. Certain materials are also rustproof, stick-resistant, easy to clean, and do not flake or react to certain foods while other materials will. The heat conductivity and energy conservation of a piece of cooking equipment is extremely important as the greater the conductivity of the material used in the construction of the equipment and the more efficiently it can retain the heat, the faster the food will cook. Some equipment is also easier to use than others, which can make food preparation faster.

Food irradiation

Food irradiation is the process of using radioactive materials to actually disinfect and preserve certain types of food. Shelf life refers to how long a particular food will last before the food spoils and begins to breed bacteria. Irradiation is important as it allows a facility to use anywhere from an extremely small amount of radiation to a relatively high dose of radiation to kill any bacteria that might be growing on a particular food item reducing the risk of foodborne illness. Irradiation is also specifically important to the shelf life of certain foods as it can help preserve certain foods by slowing their growth. Irradiation has been shown to be completely safe and poses no noticeable risk to individuals that eat the foods that it is used on, but rather acts as an effective manner of prolonging the shelf life of and killing the bacteria found on these particular foods. Some examples of foods that are commonly irradiated include apples, bananas, fish, onions, poultry, potatoes, red meats, and strawberries.

Clothing and Textiles

Wardrobe planning

An individual that is planning out his or her wardrobe should begin by considering what kinds of clothing they usually wear as well as what kinds of clothing they will need for casual, business, or other uses. For example, the president of a major corporation might need more formalwear instead of casual clothing. After the individual has come up with a basic outline of the kinds of clothing that he or she might need, the individual should take an inventory of the clothing that he or she already has to determine what types of clothing the individual may need to purchase. Once the individual has determined which types of clothing are lacking in his or her wardrobe, the individual needs to determine what factors are important for each of those types of clothing. For example, an individual searching for formalwear might be more concerned with matching colors and overall appearance than how strong the materials are. Finally, the individual can select clothing based on the factors he or she set.

Clothing selection

The four major factors that an individual might want to consider when selecting a piece of clothing include price, purpose, quality, and overall appearance. An individual that is attempting to decide on which garment to purchase may want to compare the price of a particular item that he or she is interested in to other similar items to see if the price is reasonable. The purpose of the clothing is extremely important to the consumer because if the consumer is looking for a particular type of clothing such as formalwear and the clothing is obviously intended for another purpose such as evening or casual wear the clothing will probably not suit the consumer's needs. The quality of the clothing is also extremely important because garments that are better constructed will cost the consumer less money on additional clothing or mending later. The overall appearance of the garment is important as well because the primary purpose of any garment is to help the individual convey a certain image.

Cost reduction techniques

An individual that is attempting to purchase clothing as cheaply as possible may want to start by making a detailed list of exactly what types of clothing the individual is looking for. This list should include an estimate of how many garments of each type the individual will need as well as an estimate of how much the individual is willing to spend overall. The individual should then determine the best time to actually go shopping where the individual will have the time available to compare various garments and decide which garments best suit the needs of the individual. When an individual is determining the best time to shop, the individual may also want to look online and through store circulars to get an idea of how much the garments they are looking for might cost and to see if there are any current sales. Finally, the individual may want to check a variety of stores, such as second-hand and discount stores, to compare prices and find the best deal.

Clothing construction

The three universal concepts that an individual should consider when attempting to determine the quality of any garment include whether or not the garment is functional, whether or not the garment is inconspicuous, and whether or not the garment is durable. A garment is functional simply if an individual can wear it and move in it freely without difficulty or fear of damaging the garment. Inconspicuous refers to the fact that there are no apparent flaws in the garment and that the garment was assembled using techniques to hide any stitching or seams that should not be showing. Finally, a garment is durable if the garment was constructed with strong high-quality materials and the seams and stitching seem to have been put in correctly and hold together.

Ready-made garments

Some of the factors that would indicate that a ready-made garment is well-constructed include that the fabric is used and put together correctly, the various colors, fibers, and designs appear to go together well, the garment appears to have a smooth appearance, and there are no obvious loose threads. Well-constructed garments should also have a seam allowance of ½ an inch or more, which means simply that there should be at least ½ an inch between the edge of one material and the seam that stitches that material to the second material. These are all very simple elements of the overall construction of a garment, but colors and designs that do not appear to go together correctly as well as loose threads on a garment usually indicate that the garment may have been put together incorrectly. If the garment does not have a smooth appearance or the seam allowances are less than ½ an inch it is also likely that the garment will not hold together as well.

Well-constructed garments

Some of the factors indicating whether a garment is well-constructed are:

- The belt has well-finished ends, is made out of a durable material, and has a buckle that appears to be well-attached and closes the belt appropriately.
- Both the right and left sides of the collar appear to be the same shape and size; has smooth curved edges and sharp flat points, and lays flat or sits correctly. It is also important that the under part of the collar does not show and that there does not appear to be a large number of extra unnecessary seams across the collar.
- The neckline is the same on both sides and matches correctly and does not appear to be bulky; facings are flat and have stitches that are not obvious.
- Darts are smooth and pressed in the appropriate direction, placed in positions that improve the overall appearance of the garment, and each dart is the same size and shape. The direction that a dart should be pressed towards depends on the type of dart as vertical darts should be pressed towards the center of the garment and horizontal darts should be pressed towards the bottom of the garment.
- The hem is flat, hangs smoothly and parallel to the floor, and the edge of the hem is smooth and secure with no loose threads. The seams of the hem should be pressed and concealed as much as possible. It is also important that the hem is the appropriate width and length for the individual that

is planning on wearing the garment.

- Buttons are attached securely, the buttons are the appropriate size to fit through the button hole and stay secure once through the hole, and the buttons are placed evenly. The buttons should also be stitched starting and ending at the bottom of the button.
- Buttonholes are placed evenly and are even in width and length, the buttonholes are the correct size, and the buttonholes lay flat and are stitched correctly. The edge of the garment that has the buttonholes should also be interfaced and buttonholes should be cut on grain at points of strain and carefully stitched to make sure that the buttonhole is secure and does not cause the garment to come apart.

Well-fitting garments

Some of the factors that indicate that a garment fits correctly include that the garment is comfortable and easy for the individual to move in, each part of the garment such as the neckline and waistline sits properly, and the garment lies flat. Garments that fit correctly should also have a smooth appearance without wrinkles and should not have any folds in the fabric other than folds that are part of the design of the garment. It is important that a garment fits an individual correctly because the individual needs to be able to function in the garment and the garment needs to fulfill the purpose that it was intended for and give the individual a certain look. A garment that does not fit correctly will usually be unable to convey the image the individual wishes to convey if the garment does not look right and the individual will not be able to function

normally if he or she is having difficulty moving in the garment.

Elements of design

There are four basic elements that make up the design of any garment, which are color, shape or form, texture, and line.

- The color refers to the shade of the garment, such as red or blue, and how bright or dull and how light or dark that shade is.
- Shape or form refers specifically to whether a garment or detail is flat or has a more three dimensional appearance. Shape refers to garments that specifically appear to be flat such as a T-shirt lying on a table while form refers to garments that have depth to them such as a wedding gown that an individual is wearing.
- The texture of a garment simply refers to how the garment feels such as rough, soft, course, silky, etc.
- The lines of a garment refer to the seams and lines that make up the fabric and any designs present in the garment.

The elements of design are important because they allow an individual that is attempting to construct a garment or to select a garment to understand the basic parts that make up a design. An individual that understands these parts can determine what actually makes a garment look good and what sorts of garments will go well together. The elements of design may not be as important if an individual is not concerned with the garment's overall appearance and is simply looking for a comfortable piece of clothing, but understanding these elements can be

- 58 -

extremely useful when an individual is attempting to improve their overall appearance. Ultimately, these elements are the basic components that make up a garment and determine whether or not that garment will give the right look when used with other garments.

Principles of design

There are five basic principles that are used in the construction of a garment to make its design more appealing, which are balance, emphasis, proportion, rhythm, and unity.

- A garment is <u>balanced</u> if both the left and ride sides of the garment appear to be similar to each other, but this does not necessarily mean that both sides are actually the same. In fact, there are two different types of balance that an individual might find when examining a garment, which are symmetrical balance and asymmetrical balance. For a garment to have symmetrical balance both sides of the garment actually have to sit at the same level and the parts on one side of the centerline of the garment have to be an exact mirror of the other side. On the other hand, a garment has asymmetrical balance if both sides are not physically identical, but are similar enough that the individual believes that both sides seem to have the same "weight." Balance is extremely important to the overall appearance of a garment because a garment that has parts that do not appear to be evenly positioned on both sides will not look as appealing.
- The <u>emphasis</u> of a garment refers to any designs, details, or parts of the garment that draw people's attention to the garment. Emphasis is important because the overall purpose of using the principles and elements of design are to create a certain appearance. To create any appearance, you first have to gain the attention of other people so the parts of the design that draw people's attention to the garment are extremely important. The emphasis of a design can be virtually anything from the use of a bright color or subtle form to an intricate image such as an ivy vine that wraps its way around the garment. However, any individual attempting to decide whether the emphasis of a garment is effective should consider whether or not it fulfills its purpose of drawing attention without being too flashy or gaudy. This is because garments that place too much emphasis on flashy and gaudy features are usually unappealing.
- A design is correctly proportioned if the attributes of the various parts of a garment such as their size, shape, and color seem to be correct when compared with each other or the garment as a whole. <u>Proportion</u> in some ways is similar to the design principle of balance as it is how the various images, lines, and other attributes of the garment appear to fit the garment when they are compared with one another. For example, a garment that has several roses of a similar size evenly spaced on it would probably be considered correctly proportioned. However, a garment with one enormous rose on it and several other roses of differing sizes placed randomly across the garment would probably be considered

incorrectly proportioned as the roses do not seem to relate well with one another. Proportion also refers to how those individual design elements relate to the garment as a whole so an enormous image of a rose that covers the entire garment is usually not proportional to the garment and will therefore appear to be overwhelming and unappealing.

- The rhythm of a design refers to any feature that causes an individual to look at one part of a design and then leads that individual to look at another part of a design. If a garment employs the design technique of rhythm, the overall design will have a basic sense of flow where one part of the design seems to flow into the next and leads the viewer's attention to the next detail in the design. Repeating patterns or colors that cause the viewer to focus on the pattern and then follow the details of the pattern along the garment are the most common way of accomplishing a sense of rhythm in a design. Rhythm is important because it is a useful technique for not only drawing people's attention to a garment, but also for keeping their attention on the garment. Some garments may have a rhythmic quality to a part of the design that is not necessarily the emphasis of the garment, but rather a way of causing onlookers to look at the complete garment rather than just the emphasis.

- Finally, the unity of a design is when a garment looks appropriate after all of the parts of the design have been put together. Unity is a state that is achieved when all of the parts of a garment seem to look right on a particular person when each of those parts are brought together. For unity to be achieved, all of the elements of the design including the design's color, lines, shape or form, and texture have to coordinate to create the look that the individual is attempting to achieve. If the elements of the garment and any other clothing that the individual is wearing do not appear to go with each other, the overall garment will not create a sense of unity and will not be able to convey the image that the individual had intended. Ultimately, unity is the end result of the garment that is achieved when all of the other principles and elements of the design are brought together to create the desired image.

Stain removal

The best way for an individual to remove a stain from a garment in most cases is to take a clean cloth, wet it with cold water, and blot the stain with the cloth starting from the outside of the stain and moving towards the center. The individual should start trying to remove the stain as soon as possible and should not use hot water or rub at the stain as these techniques can cause the stain to set into the fabric or spread. This technique will work with most stains on most garments, but should be used sparingly, if at all, on non-washable fabrics. Regardless of what type of garment and what kind of stain the individual is dealing with, it can be a good idea to check the care instructions before attempting to remove the stain.

Garment cleaning

The two primary techniques that an individual can use to clean a garment are home washing and dry cleaning.

- Home washing simply refers to an individual either washing a garment by hand or machine-washing a garment using some combination of water and detergent to remove dirt and stains from his or her clothing.
- Dry-cleaning refers to a process where the garment is cleaned using solvents and other chemicals that are heated and very little if any water is used. It is important that an individual determines the appropriate technique to clean a garment as certain materials may shrink or disintegrate if they are washed with water while other garments may react poorly to the solvents used in dry cleaning. Certain types of materials also need to be washed at specific temperatures so it is also important for an individual to know if the material might be damaged by the heat involved with dry cleaning or washing a garment in hot water.

The best way for an individual to determine which technique to use in washing a particular garment is to follow the care instructions on the care label. Virtually all garments have care instructions written by the manufacturer attached to the garment that explain what techniques are best to use in washing the garment. These labels are actually required by law, but in some instances, the care label may have been removed or accidentally left off the garment and the individual will have to determine what techniques to use based on the materials of the garment. Stronger materials such as cottons, linens, polyesters, and stronger silks can be machine-washed in warm water without a problem. Garments that are made out of materials that may shrink or pick up colors such as nylon should be washed in cold water rather than warmer water. Garments that contain materials that are more delicate such as most acetates, acrylics, and most types of wool should almost always be dry-cleaned.

The washing techniques that the following care instructions identify:

- Garments that can be machine-washed can be cleaned using any normal method of washing and drying unless specifically stated otherwise. This means that machine-washable garments can be cleaned by hand, by using a washing machine and dryer, dry-cleaned, cleaned by commercial laundry services, or any other reasonable method unless the care instructions state otherwise.
- Home launder means that a garment can be cleaned by any method except for commercial laundry services as the procedures frequently used in commercial laundering may damage the garment.
- No chlorine bleach means that the individual can use bleaches that do not contain chlorine such as oxygen bleaches but chlorine bleaches may damage or discolor the garment. No bleach simply means no bleach of any kind should be used to wash the garment.
- Cold wash/cold rinse simply that the garment should be washed in cold water, warm wash/warm rinse means the garment should be washed in warm water, and hot wash means the garment should be washed in hot water.

- No spin is only applicable if the garment is being machine-washed, but it means that the garment should be removed before the final spin cycle to avoid damaging the garment.
- When the care instructions indicate delicate cycle, gentle cycle, durable cycle, or permanent press cycle, the instructions are referring to the cycle setting on a washing machine that should be used to minimize the chances of damage to the garment. Stronger materials can usually be washed on any setting, but some materials are more delicate and therefore more likely to be damaged during longer cycles where the inside of the washing machine is spinning faster.
- Wash separately means simply that the garment should not be washed with other garments or should be washed with garments of a similar color. Garments usually need to be washed separately because the colors in the garment are likely to run and damage other clothing or the garment is likely to pick up colors from other clothing.
- Hand-wash means that a garment should not be machine-washed, but it can be washed by hand or dry-cleaned. Garments that should be hand-washed usually have this particular instruction because the garment is extremely delicate. Garments that need to be hand-washed usually need to be washed in warm water. Hand-wash only means that the garment should solely be washed by hand and dry cleaning or any other method should not be used.
- Dry-clean only means that the garment should not be cleaned by a commercial laundry service or a home method and should only be dry-cleaned. No dry clean means simply that dry cleaning should not be used.
- Tumble-dry means that that garment can be dried using a normal dryer and the temperature that should be used such as low, medium, or high usually follows the "tumble-dry" instruction. Drip-dry means that the individual should not use a dryer, but rather hang the garment while it is still wet and let it dry.

Fiber, yarn, thread, fabric

Fibers are thin filaments similar to thread usually found in plants or the fur of animals. Fibers can also be man-made filaments that are formed by forcing chemicals through small holes called spinnerets. These fibers are used for a variety of different purposes including the construction of yarn, thread and fabric.
Yarn is a collection of long lengths of tightly spun fibers that are usually used in the production of fabric.
Thread is a collection of long, thin lengths of fibers that are used for sewing two fabrics together.
Fabric is a material constructed by weaving or knitting yarn together to form a type of cloth. Fabrics come in a variety of different colors, textures, and appearances and have a wide range of uses including being used to make carpeting, cleaning products such as towels, and clothing.

Fibers

The two major types of fibers that are used in the construction of fabrics are natural fibers and synthetic fibers.

- 62 -

Natural fibers are simply any fibers that are taken from plants or animals while synthetic fibers are fibers that are created in a laboratory or factory through the use of chemicals. Each fiber has its own distinct characteristics, but there are many similarities between the characteristics of naturally made fibers and many similarities between the characteristics of each fiber that is man-made.

Synthetic fibers are often similar in certain ways to natural fibers as researchers often base the synthetic fiber on a natural fiber for which they want to make a stronger or less expensive alternative. However, synthetic fibers often react very differently under certain conditions such as heat and sunlight than natural fibers so it can be extremely important for an individual to understand the differences between synthetic and natural fibers.

Acetate fibers are synthetic fibers that are soft, smooth, dry, weak, lustrous, and heat-sensitive. Acetate fibers are used in the construction of a variety of fabrics including satins and taffetas primarily to give the fabric a more shiny, lustrous look. Fabrics that are made from acetate fibers are also more resistant to shrinking.

Acrylic fibers are synthetic fibers that are soft, lightweight, resilient, and heat-sensitive. Acrylic fibers are often used as a replacement for wool as they have a very similar feel to wool. Acrylic fibers are also often used as a cheaper alternative to cashmere as they have a very similar appearance.

Cotton fibers are natural fibers that are relatively strong, soft, light sensitive, elastic, breathable, and can absorb and retain water effectively. Many fabrics are made completely out of cotton fibers or a blend of cotton fibers with other fibers such as rayon and polyester. Fabrics made from cotton fibers are usually soft and heat resistant, but are also more likely to shrink.

Flax fibers are natural fibers very similar to cotton fibers that are soft, breathable, and strong, but lack the elasticity that cotton fibers have. High-quality flax fibers are primarily used in the construction of linens. Fabrics made from flax fibers are usually similar to fabrics made from cotton and are soft and heat resistant, but are also likely to shrink.

Nylon fibers are synthetic fibers that are smooth, strong, lightweight, elastic, and lustrous. Nylon fibers are primarily used as a cheaper alternative to silk. Fabrics made from nylon are relatively inexpensive, strong, and extremely light, but will melt at high temperatures.

Polyester fibers are synthetic fibers that are strong, lightweight, resilient, and resistant to many of the conditions that might normally harm a fabric such as mildew, sunlight, harsh weather, and moths. Polyester fibers are used in a wide range of fabrics and are often used in a cotton/polyester blend.

Ramie fibers are natural fibers that are very strong, have a lustrous appearance similar to silk, and absorb and retain water effectively. However, they are also brittle, stiff, inelastic, and not very resilient. Ramie fibers are very difficult work with and are usually used in blends with other fibers such as wool to make a variety of fabrics.

Rayon fibers are synthetic fibers that have many of the same characteristics as cotton fibers and are relatively soft, smooth, strong, resistant to moths, and can retain water extremely well. Rayon fibers are used in a variety of fabrics including most types of velvet as it can imitate the feel of silk and other natural fibers.

Silk fibers are natural fibers that are extremely soft, strong, lustrous, and absorb and retain water effectively. They are also resistant to mildew and moths. Silk fibers are used in the construction of a wide range of fabrics such as chiffon, organza, and taffeta because of the silk's soft feel and extremely lustrous appearance.

Wool fibers are natural fibers that normally are coarse, relatively strong, resilient, and can retain water well. Wool fibers are commonly used in a variety of fabrics such as flannel because wool fibers usually improve a fabric's ability to retain heat. Most types of wool have a sort of scratchy feel to them, which is why many individuals believe that they are allergic to wool, but some wool fabrics such as cashmere can actually be very soft.

Making fabric

A textile manufacturer that is attempting to make a particular type of fabric would begin by acquiring the appropriate fibers from plant or animal sources or manufacturing the fibers that are needed for that particular fabric. The manufacturer would then convert those fibers, usually through a process called spinning where the fibers are spun together tightly, into yarn. The yarn is then knitted or woven together by hand or by machine to form the fabric. The fabric is then put through a series of treatments that are designed to improve the overall appearance and feel of the fabric. These treatments include processes such as dyeing, which the manufacturer would use to achieve the desired color for the fabric unless the natural or plant fibers are that color already. Finally, the fabric is usually treated with a series of finishing chemicals that are designed to improve the fabric's resistance to certain harmful conditions such as weather or sunlight.

Housing

Housing functions

The primary purpose for any type of housing is to act as a form of shelter for an individual or a group of people. Shelter in this context primarily refers to protecting the individual or group from harsh weather such as rain, snow, extreme heat, extreme cold, harsh winds, extensive exposure to UV radiation, or any other conditions that might prove unpleasant or harmful. Housing can also provide security to the individual or family by making it more difficult for harmful things, such as animals, insects, unscrupulous individuals, and other threats, to actually get to the individual or group and their belongings. In some cases, housing can also serve as a location for individuals to do business and work from or the house itself can even act as a symbol of the wealth and status of the individual or family.

Security

Security can be extremely important for an individual or group that is wealthy, well known, or in general just at high risk of being victimized by thieves or other criminals. A home can provide a wide range of protective measures to help keep the individual or family and their belongings safe including locks on doors and windows, burglar alarms, and fire alarms and carbon monoxide detectors to warn the family of potentially deadly threats. Some homes, especially homes that are in high-risk areas, contain a large number of personal assets, or house individuals who are at high risk due to their social status, may also have additional security measures in place. These measures include security features such as stronger locks like deadbolts, security cameras, and gates and checkpoints for gated communities or for individuals at extremely high risk such as high-ranking politicians.

Home business

There are a number of major advantages usually associated with an individual or group running their business from home. Probably the most important advantage of running a home based business is the fact that the individual or group can usually significantly reduce their overhead costs as a result of a single building being used for both business and living purposes. These overhead costs that can be reduced include expenses related to transportation, business clothing, furnishing the office, maintenance, mortgage or rent, taxes, and other similar expenses that an individual or group may not have to spend as much on if they own one building instead of two separate buildings. Some of the other major advantages of running a home based business include that the individual has a more flexible schedule, has the ability to put most of the time that would be spent commuting to better use, and the individual is readily available to carry out their domestic responsibilities.

For an individual to be able to work successfully and efficiently in any environment, he or she usually needs a somewhat private place to work that is relatively free from distractions. The individual, regardless of what type of business he or she is attempting to perform, will also require a certain amount of time to accomplish the work he or she needs to do and the necessary equipment to perform that work. Some of the equipment an individual may require for his or her home business include a computer, printer, fax machine,

- 65 -

telephone, computer programs appropriate to the type of work to be performed, etc. It is also important that an individual is able to find the storage space necessary for any equipment that the business will need to function appropriately.

The single largest problem that home business owners are usually faced with is a conflict arising between the needs of the family and the needs of the business. Every business has its own distinct needs and those needs can often be difficult to achieve in a home setting as a conflict can arise between the space, time, and equipment that the family needs and the space, time, and equipment that the business needs. For example, a child or other family member may need the space or the equipment, such as a computer, to complete their homework at the same time that the individual is using it to work. On the other hand, the children of the family may not need the computer, but instead need the individual to feed them or help them with their homework, which can distract the individual from the tasks he or she needs to complete. Any equipment purchased specifically for the business will also require space that the family was probably already using for another purpose.

Status symbol

The major reason that a home can act as a status symbol for an individual or family that lives in a particular home is because of the enormous financial investment that is normally necessary. Regardless of the type of home that the individual or family lives in, actually purchasing or leasing a home is usually the single largest expense that any individual or family will encounter during their lives. As a result, the home of an individual or family can act as an indication of the overall wealth that a family possesses. This means that the larger and more luxurious the house that the individual or family owns, the greater the amount of wealth that the individual or family must have had available to have acquired that home. Since wealth is commonly associated with the status of an individual, the type of home that an individual or family lives in acts as a way of distinguishing how much wealth the individual or family has and therefore indicates their status as well.

Types of housing

The two major types of housing that an individual or family might live in are houses and apartments. A house is an entire building that the primary purpose of that building is for an individual or family to reside in it. An apartment is actually a section of a building that has been split into units and the primary purpose of each particular unit is for an individual or single family to reside in that unit. The major difference is that a building is considered a house if the whole building belongs to one individual, family, or several families that share the entire building or at least most of the building. On the other hand, a building is considered to be an apartment building or a complex if it contains separate sections or units that each allow a separate family to live on their own without sharing a large portion of the building.

The three major types of houses found in the United States are single-family houses, townhouses, and semi-detached houses. A single-family house is simply any building used as a home for residential use that is separate from any other buildings. Townhouses are a series of buildings where all of the buildings share both of their side walls with the buildings on each side with the exception of the houses at the ends of the row, which only share one wall. Semi-detached houses are two residential buildings that share only a single wall and have empty space on their other side. These three major types of houses are basically defined by how much space is available around the building. A single-family home has space available on all sides, a semi-detached house has space clear in front, behind, and on one side of the house, and townhouses with the exception of the townhouses on the end of the row only have space in front and behind the house.

Types of apartments

The most common types of apartments found in the United States are single or multi-bedroom apartments and studio apartments. Single or multi-bedroom apartments are units that have one or more bedrooms that are separated from the rest of the unit. Studio apartments are units that have one large room that makes up the entire unit and performs the functions of a bedroom, living room, dining room, kitchen, and any other rooms that the unit's tenants require. Studio apartments and single or multi-bedroom apartments are usually rented, but it is becoming more and more common for apartments to be sold to consumers as condominiums or cooperatives. Regardless of whether an apartment is rented or purchased, studio apartments are almost always less expensive than multi-bedroom apartments and the price of the unit increases significantly with each extra separate bedroom attached to the unit.

Condominium and cooperative

A condominium, also known as a condo, is a type of apartment ownership where an individual has purchased complete ownership of a single unit, but has shared ownership of certain common areas and common expenses associated with the building. This means that the individual living in the condo owns the unit and is responsible for all of the expenses associated with that unit, but shares the rest of the building and the expenses associated with the remainder of the building. A cooperative, also known as a co-op, is a type of apartment where an individual owns shares in a corporation and that corporation owns the entire building. The individual that owns the shares has the right to live in a particular unit within the building as long as they follow certain guidelines set by the corporation.

The major difference between a condominium and a cooperative is that a condo owner actually owns the unit and shares ownership of the building, while a co-op owner does not actually own the unit or the building, but rather owns part of a corporation and that corporation owns the building. The owner of a condo, by paying condo fees and discussing problems with a condo association, directly shares the decisions and expenses related to the upkeep of the building. A co-op owner, on the other hand, is not directly responsible for the expenses and problems of the building as the corporation that owns the building handles these expenses and problems using the funds they gather from the rent or subscription fees paid for the co-op owners.

Housing payment methods

The two most common methods that an individual or family might use to pay for their housing are renting, also known as leasing, and purchasing the house through a mortgage or loan. Renting is when an individual does not actually own the house or apartment, but rather pays a

- 67 -

monthly fee for the use of that house or apartment. An individual that takes out a mortgage on a particular type of housing, on the other hand, actually purchases that house or apartment using the money acquired from a loan and each monthly payment is to pay back the institution that loaned the individual or family the necessary money. These two types of payment are basically distinguished by the owner of the property as an individual who rents does not own the property, but rather pays a fee to the owner for using the property while an individual with a mortgage actually owns the property that they live in.

Renting

The two major advantages of renting housing rather than purchasing housing are that renting is usually less expensive in terms of monthly payments and the individual or family does not have to be concerned with costs associated with maintaining the building. A renter or lessee does not actually own the building and only has to pay whatever fee the building's owner has set for that particular unit regardless of any work that the rest of the building may require. For example, if the building's plumbing needs work, any cost that is associated with repairing the plumbing is actually the responsibility of the building's owner and not the responsibility of the apartment's tenant. The major disadvantage of renting is that the individual, in most cases, does not actually gain any long-term advantage from paying rent because each rent payment is not actually being put towards purchasing the property.

Purchasing

The major advantage of purchasing housing rather than renting is that the individual or family actually owns the property and can sell that property at a later time. Each monthly payment is actually going towards paying off the loan that was used to purchase the property and the individual can decide to sell that property at any point and keep any money that is leftover after paying the bank back. An individual who is renting can leave the apartment at any time, but usually will receive no benefit from the money he or she had already paid while living there. On the other hand, the two major disadvantages of purchasing a home are that the monthly payments are usually higher than what an individual renting a home would pay and the individual or family is responsible for all or at least part of the expenses associated with maintaining the home.

Renting versus purchasing

An individual that is attempting to decide whether to rent or purchase a particular type of housing should base his or her decision primarily on the individual's income. This can be done by estimating how much buying a piece of property will cost the individual per month, how much renting will cost the individual per month, and the individual's monthly income. If the individual has the money available to put a reasonable down payment on a piece of property that the individual is interested in and has the income to make the monthly mortgage payments on the property without a problem, buying is usually the better option. This is because purchasing a piece of property, unlike renting, is an investment that can be sold to offer at least some financial return to the individual. On the other hand, if the individual cannot afford to make a reasonable down payment and the monthly mortgage payments are more than the individual can comfortably afford, renting may be a better option.

- 68 -

An individual or family that is attempting to determine which buildings should be considered should begin by determining how much the individual or family can afford to spend on housing. Purchasing or even renting housing is always a major investment and the individual or family needs to make sure that they have the funds available to make the payments necessary. Next, the individual or family should determine what attributes of the house or apartment are important to the individual or family such as where should it be located, how big should it be, how much storage space does the individual or family need, how much yard space, etc. Once the individual or family has made a list of all of the things that should be in their ideal house or apartment, they should then begin looking for houses or apartments that are within their price range and best suit their needs.

Neighborhood

Some of the most important factors regarding the surrounding area that an individual might want to consider include the current state of the neighborhood, how accessible the property is, and the current state of local schools and recreation. The current state of the neighborhood refers to factors such as the overall appearance of the neighborhood, the traffic and noise level, the number of children living in the area, parking, zoning or other regulations and restrictions, and the level of police, fire, and community involvement in the neighborhood. The accessibility of a piece of property refers to its location and how close it is to stores, public transportation, major roads and highways, and how close it is to where the individual or family's providers work. The current state of local schools and recreation refers mainly to how close is the house or apartment to these facilities,

how well maintained are these facilities, and the reputation surrounding these facilities.

Interior design

Interior design is the process of planning out the best way possible to construct a particular room, series of rooms, or an entire house. The primary purpose of interior design is simply to make each room both as functional and as appealing as possible. Interior designers usually consider seven basic elements of design when attempting to plan out how to make a particular room appealing, which include color, texture, pattern, line, shape, form, and mass. The functionality of a room is usually first planned out by determining the purpose that a room will serve. Once the interior designer knows the purpose of the room, he or she can then create a floor plan of how the room or rooms will fit into the rest of the house and of how the room itself will be organized to fulfill the intended purpose.

Floor plans

Some of the factors that an individual should consider when designing a floor plan include what size should the room or rooms be, what furniture needs to go in each room, how often will each room be used, and the traffic patterns of the room. The individual should also consider how many electrical outlets does the room need, how much lighting is necessary for the room, and does the room have any special requirements necessary to fulfill the purpose of the room. For example, a photographer that is planning on adding on a darkroom would probably need a small room that is located away from outside walls and windows, lets in virtually no light, has access to a number of electrical outlets and countertops for developing equipment, and sinks for rinsing film. A well-designed floor plan is important because it allows an individual to eliminate problems such as not enough space for storage, furniture, or equipment, not enough light, not enough access to power, etc.

Traffic patterns

An individual that is attempting to analyze the traffic patterns of a particular room should consider the purpose of the room, the location of the room in relation to other rooms, the number of people that will be using the room, and the ease of movement in the room. The traffic patterns of a room refer basically to how many people are moving into, through, and around that room and how easy it is for them to make those movements. For example, a room that is near the center of a house and connects two rooms on different sides should have a clear, straight path entering and exiting each connecting room. This means that people walking through the room should be able to walk straight through without having to walk around couches, tables, chairs, or other furniture that is blocking their path. A room with a well-planned traffic pattern will also allow people to get to every part of the room without climbing over or walking around furniture unnecessarily.

Education

Educational goals

The Association for Career and Technical Education has identified nine goals commonly associated with education. These nine goals are to:

- Improve the overall quality of life for individuals and families.
- Help individuals and families become responsible members of society.
- Encourage healthy eating habits, nutrition, and lifestyles.
- Improve how individuals and families manage their resources.
- Help individuals and families balance their personal, family, and work roles.
- Teach individuals better problem-solving techniques.
- Encourage personal and career development.
- Teach individuals to successfully function as both consumers and providers.
- Recognize human worth and take responsibility for ones own actions.

Quality of life

The first of the nine goals established for education is to improve the overall quality of life for individuals and families, which is also the primary mission that all of the goals aid in accomplishing. Education teaches people about how individuals, families, and the rest of society interact with each other and methods for improving those interactions. These methods include problem-solving techniques, common scams and problems to avoid, methods to stay healthy both physically and psychologically, and a variety of other information regarding how the individual, family, and the rest of society functions. Ultimately, the primary goal of education is to improve the quality of life by educating individuals and families in the best manner to function on a day to day basis. However, this goal is only really accomplished when the other eight goals of education are completed.

Sexual stereotypes

Eliminating sexual stereotypes is a major concern of education as it is important that an individual is able to disregard sexual stereotypes and recognize that an individual's gender does not necessarily affect the role a particular individual plays. In the early to mid 1900's, women were commonly seen as caretakers of the home and men as providers for the family. However, these roles have changed drastically over the past fifty to sixty years and it is important that individuals realize that it may not be realistically possible for women and men to play these roles any longer. For an individual or family to function appropriately, there are certain necessities that must be acquired and as the cost of living increases, it becomes more and more difficult for a single individual to provide for the entire family. As a result, both men and women need to share the caretaker and provider roles to satisfy the physiological, financial, and psychological needs of the family.

Balancing roles

It is important that an individual is able to balance his or her work and home roles because it is becoming more and more common for individuals to have to act as both caregiver and provider for the family. The ever more common presence of dual roles in society can be extremely difficult for an individual to balance as there may be instances where work-related responsibilities and family-related responsibilities conflict with one another. education attempts to teach individuals how to avoid and how to handle these conflicts through the use of successful life management tactics such as time and resources management, problem-solving and decision-making techniques, effective communication techniques, etc. education also attempts to give individuals a basic understanding of what responsibilities and qualities are necessary for the successful completion of each role so that individuals can set better priorities and find better ways to plan their lives.

Skill types

There are three types of skills and indications about whether those skills are being used effectively:

- An individual's level of affective skill refers to how effectively an individual can recognize, understand, and handle emotions, relationships, and other social interaction. Affective skills allow an individual to feel a certain emotion as a result of a certain situation or stimuli and then respond based on that emotion. Some of the factors that can be used to measure how well-developed an individual's affective skills are include determining how well the individual receives emotional stimuli and how well the individual responds to those stimuli. It is also important to determine how easy it is for the individual to acknowledge the worth of a particular situation, relationship, or individual and whether or not the individual has

an organized and well-conceived value system. An individual's ability to receive and respond to emotional stimuli can be measured by how aware the individual is of a particular stimulus, how willing the individual is to acknowledge that particular stimulus, and how focused the individual is on that stimulus. An individual's ability to assign value to a situation and uphold a value system can be measured by how motivated the individual is, how the individual behaves, and how consistent is that individual's behavior. For example, a student that always comes to class and clearly always pays attention may have well-developed affective skills.

- An individual's level of cognitive skill refers to an individual's ability to gather and understand information. Cognitive skills allow an individual to comprehend and apply knowledge that they have already gathered in other situations. Some of the factors that can be used to measure how well-developed an individual's cognitive skills are include determining the individual's ability to retain knowledge, comprehend knowledge, apply knowledge, and evaluate knowledge. An individual's ability to retain knowledge can be measured by testing the individual's ability to remember certain facts and information through exams or simply asking questions. An individual's ability to comprehend knowledge can be measured by an individual demonstrating a concept in a different form, explaining a

- 72 -

concept in more detail or simplifying a concept, or predicting a result based on a particular concept. An individual breaking a concept down into individual parts and demonstrating how those parts make up the whole can also show comprehension of a particular concept. An individual's ability to apply knowledge can be measured by an individual demonstrating that they can use a particular concept for a real-life purpose. Finally, an individual's ability to evaluate a particular piece of knowledge can be indicated by the individual showing the value of that knowledge.

- An individual's level of psychomotor skill refers to an individual's ability to control his or her physical movements as well as his or her coordination. In other words, psychomotor skills are the ability that an individual has to control his or her simple and complex motor functions. Some of the factors that can be used to measure how well-developed an individual's psychomotor skills are include how well an individual performs physical skills and acts, how precisely can the individual perform those skills or activities, and how natural do those activities seem to be for the individual. An individual's ability to use physical skills can be measured simply by how much difficulty the individual has in accomplishing a particular complex physical activity such as climbing a rope or assembling a model. How precisely the individual can perform those skills or activities can be measured by determining the quality of the end result of the individual's physical activity and how long it took the individual to reach that result. For example, if the individual has constructed a model plane, does the model look like a plane, are its wings and other parts attached correctly, how long it took to assemble, etc. Finally, an activity is natural for an individual if the individual can perform it without thinking.

Skills used everyday

It is extremely important for an individual to be able to use a combination of his or her affective, cognitive, and psychomotor skills together on a day-to-day basis as each type of skill is essential to the overall functioning of a healthy individual. An individual that has mastered his or her psychomotor skills may be in excellent physical health, but the individual's overall health as well as the health of the individual's family will suffer if the individual is unable to make effective relationships and understand basic and complex concepts. The situation is the same for an individual that can only make effective relationships or who can only understand complex concepts as it will be significantly more difficult for the individual to perform everyday functions if the individual has poor control over his or her psychomotor skills. For an individual to maintain the physical and mental health of the individual and his or her family, the individual has to be able to use a combination of different skills.

Professional organizations

Professional organizations such as the American Association of Family and Consumer Sciences, also known as the AAFCS, play an important role in

- 73 -

influencing the education of individuals in the methodology and knowledge associated with . Many of these local and national professional organizations offer seminars, courses, and publications directly to individuals and families to help them learn how to improve essential career and management skills, how to be smart consumers, give them information about proper nutrition, and information about a wide range of other topics. These professional organizations also usually offer publications, advice, and curriculum guides to teachers, professors, and other education professionals that help these professionals teach and stay informed regarding important changes to the curriculum that occur as societal norms change. These organizations also have a profound effect on family and consumer science education by influencing public policy and gathering support for programs that help educate and protect individuals and families from unsafe habits, business practices, products, and lifestyles.

Family and consumer education

Family and consumer education is a teaching discipline that attempts to teach and improve a variety of skills that are essential for the day-to-day functioning of an individual and his or her family. Family and consumer education includes educating individuals in specific topics such as family interaction, human development, nutrition, consumer economics, types of housing and housing design, textiles, parenting, appropriate cooking and handling of foods, and a variety of other topics necessary for an individual to continue functioning successfully. Family and consumer education covers information about both the physical needs of the individual and the psychological needs of the individual and puts a large emphasis on the

necessity of appropriate social interaction between the individual and the rest of society. Individuals in the family and consumer education field are teachers, professors, and other education professionals as the purpose of the discipline is to educate individuals in techniques that they can use in their daily lives to improve their overall well being.

There are several concepts that are at the core of family and consumer education, but one of the most important concepts is that families are the basic unit of society. Humans do not function well in solitary environments and therefore they usually live together in groups and the basic groups that make up society are families. Another important concept of family and consumer education is that individuals need to be life-long learners in order to develop and function appropriately. This means that each individual needs to be taught the skills necessary to gather information in the future. Finally, family and consumer education believes that individuals and families need to have an understanding of the advantages of different methods and diverse ways of thinking in order to solve any given problem.

There are a large number of methods that an educator can use to demonstrate concepts related to , but the best methods always involve promoting the students' active participation. Some examples of demonstrations that promote active participation are allowing students to use a sewing machine, having students test the qualities of various textiles to see how soft, lustrous, resilient, absorbent, etc. each material is, and having students prepare a meal. Some other examples of valid demonstration methods include comparing advertisements to find the best offer and examine common marketing tactics, allowing students to

- 74 -

visit or work-in a local day-care center, or getting students involved in local community service activities. Many of these activities not only act as an effective way of teaching students about the important concepts of , but also act as a means of testing the student's ability to apply the techniques and information that they have learned.

Occupational education

Occupational education is a teaching discipline that is similar to the standard discipline of family and consumer education, but focuses less on the skills for day-to-day living and more on how those skills can be used in the workplace. Occupational education covers information regarding skills that can commonly be applied in fields such as health services, food service, child care, hospitality, fashion design, interior design, and many other similar fields. Occupational places more emphasis on family and consumer skills that can be directly related to use in a career, such as management techniques and ethical businesses practices, than the standard family and consumer education discipline. This educational discipline ultimately takes the skills that an individual has learned from the standard discipline and shows how those skills can be applied to a career.

Community advisory committees

Community advisory committees can be extremely useful to an education professional that is attempting to determine what areas of the family and consumer science discipline a class should focus on because they offer insight into the concerns and demographics of the students. Each community has its own separate problems, concerns, and level of diversity and it is important that a family and consumer science teacher can recognize and focus on areas of concern that the students may require more improvement in than students from other communities. For example, a community that is having problems with wide spread teenage drug abuse and teenage suicide may want the community's family and consumer science teachers to focus more on avoiding substance abuse and methods of handling depression. The overall goal of a educator is to improve the overall quality of life for the students and their families and the educator cannot do that if he or she does not know what problems need to be addressed.

Some of the functions that community advisory committees perform, other than offering advice to education professionals, include assessing the performance of family and consumer science programs, assessing the performance of students with special needs, and providing equipment, technology, and resources for family and consumer science programs. These resources may include raw materials, textile samples, charts and diagrams, library books, access to computers and design software, etc. Community advisory committees also attempt to help students improve their chances of finding better jobs and careers and act as a sort of public relations department for local family and consumer science programs. Ultimately, the primary purpose of a community advisory committee is to ensure that a program has all of the resources and training necessary to achieve the program's goals and to make sure that the program is moving towards achieving those goals.

Laboratory settings

A laboratory setting can be important for an educator teaching as it offers students an opportunity to gain hands-on experience regarding a variety of skills and techniques. Many of the important areas of the discipline center around using a combination of various skills to achieve a certain end result and sometimes the best way to teach the appropriate manner of integrating these skills is through experience. A laboratory setting offers individuals a place to demonstrate and improve their skills related to the family and consumer science field where an educator can answer questions and correct mistakes. Some examples of useful laboratory settings for the field include kitchens or food science laboratories, day care centers, testing laboratories for textiles or consumer products, and many other similar settings.

Evaluating understanding

Usually, the best method that an educator can use to determine whether or not a student understands a particular concept is to see whether or not the student can actively apply the information that he or she has learned to everyday tasks. These tasks can include activities such as cooking, sewing, time management, etc. It is also possible for an educator to test a student's level of comprehension by administering written tests, assigning projects and research papers, having students design charts and diagrams, evaluating case studies and scenarios, having students keep a journal of their activities and eating habits, and many other similar methods. Which evaluation method an educator should use depends primarily on the material that the program is covering as it may be difficult for an individual to actively demonstrate their understanding of certain concepts if a laboratory setting is not available.

FCCLA

The FCCLA, which stands for the Family, Career, and Community Leaders of America, is a youth organization for students in family and consumer science education. The FCCLA offers a variety of publications and programs designed to educate people about parenting, relationships, substance abuse, teen pregnancy, teen violence, and a variety of other concerns. The primary purpose of these programs is not only to educate, but also to bring public attention to the problems that young people face and in turn gather support for programs and laws that help protect young people and their families. The FCCLA also attempts to help show students how they can improve their family and consumer science skills and apply those skills to finding careers later in life.

The FCCLA and other similar youth organizations play an important role in providing education and influencing national policy related to protecting families and consumers. However, these organizations are also important because they help make other family and consumer science programs more successful. The primary goal of any program is to improve the overall quality of life for the individual and family and the best way to do that is to get people learning about and involved in as early as possible. The students that educators are teaching now will eventually go out and start future families so it is essential that these students can learn the skills that will allow them and their families to live better lives now. The FCCLA and other similar youth organizations play an important role in not only educating people about family and consumer science concepts, but also in allowing students additional opportunities to improve and actively apply their skills.

Consumer science careers

Some of the specific careers that individuals might be able to use their family and consumer science skills in include food management, financial management, human resources, public relations, tailoring, dress-making, etc. Regardless of which career an individual chooses there is almost always some combination of skills that an individual can use both in his or her day-to-day living and in his or her career. An individual in food management can use knowledge about nutritional needs, the proper handling of food, and the temperatures and the amount of time necessary to prepare various foods. Financial advisors can use information regarding how to assess resources, determine the best way to cut costs, and determine how much an individual needs to save before retirement. Human resource and public relations managers can use their social skills and their knowledge of time management, resource management, and of human development and psychology to more effectively carry out their responsibilities. Finally, tailors and dressmakers can use their knowledge of various textiles and textile design to construct better garments.

An educator that is attempting to teach his or her students how to find the appropriate career and the skills that might be necessary for that career may want to begin by offering some examples of different careers. Some of these examples may be directly related to family and consumer science careers, but is also important that the educator identifies some careers that may not be directly related. It is important for the class to examine a diverse sampling of different careers because family and consumer science skills can be applied to virtually any setting and it is essential for an educator to teach his or her students methods of determining how various techniques can be applied. For example, a construction worker might not need to know about food, textiles, or housing design, but he or she still needs to know various problem-solving techniques. It can also be extremely useful if students can get some hands-on experience applying family and consumer science concepts to the tasks associated with various careers.

New legislation

When a new act of legislation is passed, it can often have a profound impact on the type of material that needs to be covered by education. A large part of improving the quality of life for individuals and families is warning individuals about the dangers and unethical practices that exist in the world around them. It is, however, also important that individuals understand the legal protections and rights granted to them by the various acts put into place by each state and the federal government. Since laws are constantly changing and the tactics that unscrupulous individuals and businesses use are changing as well, family and consumer science educators need to be able to adapt quickly and add information regarding new legislation to their curriculum.

Assessing student needs

The first step that an educator should take when determining the best way to meet the special needs of a student should be to determine exactly what the needs of the student are. If the student is performing poorly, the educator needs to determine whether it is because the student does not understand the material or because the student is unmotivated by the material. Each student is unique in his or her ability to learn and comprehend the material and therefore it is important for an educator to determine the cause of the student's poor performance. Once the cause has been identified, the teacher can determine how much assistance is needed. If the student's needs can be met through techniques such as one-on-one attention or assigning special projects, this is usually the best course of action. However, if the student has needs that require solutions beyond simple changes in curriculum, such as potential psychological or physiological disorders, the educator may have to discuss other options with the child's parents.

Assessment validity

The type of technique an educator should use to ensure the validity of an assessment depends on the type of assessment that is being performed. To ensure the validity of a written exam, an educator should consider using an outline of the material that has been covered by the class to design the questions that are included on the test. This allows the educator to make sure that the exam is a valid assessment of how much information the students have learned and understood rather than assessing students on material that may not truly indicate what students have learned in class. An educator that wishes to ensure the validity of a laboratory demonstration being used as an assessment should use a quality checklist to check the laboratory equipment before the demonstration and make sure to observe the students as they work. This allows the educator, to ensure that the laboratory equipment is functioning properly and that the laboratory environment remains uncontaminated by outside influences that may cause a student to fail.

Practice Test

Practice Questions

1. The process through which a person comes to think of himself or herself as a distinct person despite being a member of a family is known as
   a. collectivization.
   b. individuation.
   c. personalization.
   d. ego birth.
   e. personification.

2. In which kind of society are people more likely to live with their extended families?
   a. Modern
   b. Industrial
   c. Urban
   d. Agrarian
   e. Nomadic

3. Which of the following is NOT considered to be necessary for a person to commit emotionally to a marriage?
   a. Good self-esteem
   b. Empathy
   c. A feeling of permanence
   d. Financial stability
   e. A strong personal identity

4. Which of the following factors has no effect on job satisfaction?
   a. Having a child between the ages of 2 and 4
   b. Flexible scheduling
   c. Parenting a newborn
   d. High wages
   e. Intellectual challenge

5. What is the first step a person should take after divorce?
   a. Receive justice from the former spouse
   b. Achieve balance between being single and being a parent
   c. Accept the fact that the marriage is over
   d. Develop goals for the future
   e. Begin looking for a new partner

6. For which pair would sibling rivalry likely be greatest?
    a. Sister and brother, ages 5 and 10, respectively
    b. Sisters, ages 10 and 5
    c. Brother and sister, ages 8 and 10, respectively
    d. Brothers, ages 3 and 5
    e. Sisters, ages 4 and 8

7. Which of the following statements about marriage is false?
    a. Married men are less likely to abuse alcohol.
    b. Married women typically earn higher wages than single women.
    c. On average, married women are healthier than single women.
    d. People who have been married in the past are more likely to marry again than people who have never married.
    e. More than 90% of Americans will marry at some point.

8. In general, accepting a stepparent is hardest for
    a. preschoolers.
    b. girls around the age of eight.
    c. boys around the age of nine.
    d. adolescent boys.
    e. adolescent girls.

9. Which of the following statements about families is false?
    a. The content rather than the style of family communication is important.
    b. Families tend to make decisions that maintain the current state of affairs.
    c. Members of a family are likely to struggle with the same sorts of problems in life.
    d. Families change in response to pressures from the environment.
    e. It is impossible to understand the members of a family without understanding the family as a whole.

10. According to John Gottman, which of the following is the best response to criticism by a spouse?
    a. Defensiveness
    b. Stonewalling
    c. Reasoned argument
    d. Humor
    e. Acceptance

11. The greatest amount of variation between people of the same age is found during
    a. Infancy
    b. Early adolescence
    c. Early childhood
    d. Adulthood
    e. Late adolescence

12. When two children have a dispute and agree to settle it according to their mother's opinion, they are engaging in
    a. Arbitration
    b. Conciliation
    c. Mediation
    d. Negotiation
    e. Restorative justice

13. In general, when a mother works,
    a. her daughters are less independent.
    b. her unsupervised sons are less successful at school.
    c. her children have more self-esteem.
    d. it is not important for both parents to have a positive attitude about the arrangement.
    e. she is less satisfied with her life.

14. Which of the following is an assumption of structured family therapy?
    a. The life of a family is a series of actions and reactions.
    b. Family members tend to become locked in their roles.
    c. During times of conflict, family members will take sides to consolidate power.
    d. Bad behavior persists when it is reinforced.
    e. Family problems are caused by negative projection.

15. What is one drawback of inpatient treatment for alcoholism?
    a. It is rarely effective.
    b. It does not include a twelve-step program.
    c. It enables the patient to continue drinking while receiving treatment.
    d. It is expensive.
    e. It requires a personal commitment from the patient.

16. According to Piaget's model, the ability to imagine the mental lives of others emerges during the
    a. formal operational stage.
    b. concrete operational stage.
    c. primary socialization stage.
    d. preoperational stage.
    e. sensorimotor stage.

17. Role strain is exemplified by
    a. a public speaker who cultivates her expertise.
    b. a new teacher who struggles to maintain authority in the classroom.
    c. a person whose parents die.
    d. a child who imagines what it would be like to be a police officer.
    e. a substitute teacher who waits tables on the weekend.

18. Which of the following people is most likely to have an IQ of 125?
    a. A fourteen year-old with the mental age of a ten year-old
    b. A five year-old with the mental age of an eight year-old
    c. A ten year-old with the mental age of a seven year-old
    d. An eight year-old with the mental age of a twelve year-old
    e. An eight year-old with the mental age of a ten year-old

19. A student whose interest level and performance have steadily declined admits to his teacher that he is depressed. Unfortunately, the student is not yet willing to do anything to remedy this problem. In which stage of the transtheoretical model of change is this student?
    a. Action
    b. Maintenance
    c. Preparation/commitment
    d. Contemplation
    e. Precontemplation

20. Starting at about nine months, an infant will begin nonsensically imitating adult speech, a process known as
    a. telegraphic speech.
    b. holophrastic speech.
    c. cooing.
    d. deep structuring.
    e. echolalia.

21. What is the major criticism of Levinson's "seasons" of life model?
    a. It overstates the importance of the mid-life crisis.
    b. It is too idealized.
    c. It ignores the last years of life.
    d. It suggests that life transitions are made unconsciously.
    e. It discounts the influence of parents.

22. Which of the following is NOT a warning sign of teen depression?
    a. Sudden interest in a new hobby
    b. Aloofness
    c. Fatigue
    d. A change in sleep patterns
    e. Rapid weight change

23. Students who excel in math receive different treatment than students who excel in English. This is an example of
    a. vertical socialization.
    b. horizontal socialization.
    c. resocialization.
    d. anticipatory socialization.
    e. desocialization.

24. Which of the following is NOT one of the areas of emotional intelligence?
    a. Self-awareness
    b. Empathy
    c. Personal motivation
    d. Thrift
    e. Altruism

25. Which of the following statements about teen pregnancy is false?
    a. The United States has the lowest rate of teen pregnancy in North America.
    b. The rate of teen pregnancy is higher among Hispanics and African-Americans.
    c. Teenage mothers are less likely to complete high school.
    d. Teen pregnancy rates have decreased over the past twenty years.
    e. Teenage parents earn less money over the course of their lives.

26. An effective time management plan
    a. encourages students to do their most difficult tasks first.
    b. eliminates every possible distraction.
    c. includes time for meals.
    d. eschews lists.
    e. will be the same for every student.

27. Creating a list of things to do is less necessary
    a. when children are teething.
    b. when both parents work in the home.
    c. when a daily routine has been established.
    d. when children are in school.
    e. when both parents work outside the home.

28. Which of Hersey and Blanchard's leadership styles emphasizes the performance of tasks and ignores the development of positive relationships?
    a. Selling
    b. Delegating
    c. Supporting
    d. Telling
    e. Participating

29. What is the best method for a family to decide on a vacation destination?
    a. One parent decides
    b. Ideas are thrown into a hat and selected at random
    c. Children decide
    d. Discussion, then a final decision by parents
    e. Vote

30. The best way to limit a child's television time is to
    a. take away privileges until the child submits.
    b. tell the child that television will rot his brain.
    c. ignore the issue.
    d. suggest that the child go outside.

e. set a timer and turn the television off when the alarm sounds.

31. A group will often make more extreme decisions than any one member would make independently. This phenomenon is known as
    a. organizational conflict.
    b. group polarization.
    c. social facilitation.
    d. groupthink.
    e. social loafing.

32. The members of a family are more likely to be motivated when
    a. they are forced to commit to a goal.
    b. a goal is well defined.
    c. they believe that their work is inherently good, regardless of any tangible reward.
    d. they do not evaluate their own performance.
    e. they feel as if they are working harder than other members.

33. A compressed workweek
    a. decreases the amount of time spent at work every day.
    b. is made up of 5 eight-hour days.
    c. improves employee satisfaction.
    d. tends to diminish performance.
    e. is especially beneficial for employees who work at home.

34. What is the first step a person should take toward eliminating wasted time?
    a. Keeping a log of how time is spent
    b. Resolving to sleep less
    c. Purchasing efficient home appliances
    d. Using an egg timer
    e. Focusing on one's most important tasks

35. A five year-old is probably too young to
    a. clean up spills with a sponge.
    b. sweep a wooden floor.
    c. dust shelves.
    d. mop the kitchen floor.
    e. put away toys.

36. The proper decision-making process begins by
    a. defining the problem to be solved.
    b. listing various solutions.
    c. researching potential solutions.
    d. assembling a team to solve the problem.
    e. estimating the cost of solving the problem.

37. When making a schedule, children should be encouraged to
    I. include some free time.
    II. place the hardest tasks first.
    III. block out long stretches for completing all homework.
    a. I only
    b. II only
    c. III only
    d. I and II
    e. II and III

38. Drop-in child care is useful when
    a. parents have very little money.
    b. a family's regular child care provider is unavailable.
    c. a family is away from home.
    d. a child has special needs.
    e. a child is in school.

39. What is one disadvantage of dealing with consumer finance companies?
    a. They do not loan money for very many purposes.
    b. They provide different rates of interest depending on the client's credit record.
    c. They help consumers purchase goods they could not otherwise afford.
    d. They tend to charge high interest rates.
    e. They do not accept property as security.

40. What type of business is the most common employer of high-school students?
    a. Grocery stores
    b. Movie theaters
    c. Theme parks
    d. Clothing stores
    e. Restaurants

41. Borrowers with a poor credit rating will not be eligible for a bank's
    a. prime rate.
    b. savings deposits.
    c. demand deposits.
    d. deposit insurance.
    e. certificates of deposit.

42. Which of the following statements about daycare is true?
    a. Children in daycare tend to be less aggressive.
    b. It is not necessary to establish the parent-child bond before beginning daycare.
    c. Children not in daycare tend to make friends more easily.
    d. The value of daycare is not related to the quality of the supervision.
    e. Children in daycare are better at articulating their desires.

43. Which of the following was NOT one of the consumer rights asserted by Presidents Kennedy and Nixon during the 1960s?
   a. Right to a safe product
   b. Right to affordability
   c. Right to redress
   d. Right to be heard
   e. Right to be informed

44. According to personal finance experts, what is the maximum percentage of income a family should spend on housing?
   a. 5%
   b. 50%
   c. 10%
   d. 25%
   e. 35%

45. Which of the following represents a discretionary expense?
   a. Textbook
   b. Rent
   c. DVD
   d. Groceries
   e. Heating oil

46. What is the typical interval for a personal budget?
   a. One day
   b. One week
   c. One month
   d. Six months
   e. One year

47. Denise has a credit card with an APR of 4.5%. If she has an average balance of $2500 throughout the year, how much interest will accrue?
   a. $25.00
   b. $112.50
   c. $450.00
   d. $450.50
   e. $2612.50

48. It is NOT a good idea to
   a. allow a child to visit a daycare center before his or her first official day there.
   b. ask daycare providers how toilet training is handled.
   c. allow a child to bring his favorite blanket or stuffed animal to daycare.
   d. visit less than three daycare providers before selecting one.
   e. have a positive discussion with a child who is about to begin daycare.

49. Which type of corporate bond is secured only by the assets and earnings of the corporation?
    a. Collateral trust bond
    b. Mortgage bond
    c. Sinking-fund bond
    d. Convertible bond
    e. Debenture bond

50. What is the major benefit of vitamin A?
    a. It helps form new cells.
    b. It helps protect the body from disease.
    c. It can increase a person's concentration and alertness.
    d. It can give a person healthy hair and skin.
    e. It enables muscle contraction.

51. From which food group should the most daily servings be taken?
    a. Bread, cereal, rice, and pasta
    b. Milk, yogurt, and cheese
    c. Fats, oils, and sweets
    d. Vegetables
    e. Meat, poultry, fish, eggs, dry beans, and nuts

52. The daily values listed on food packaging assume that
    a. the food will be shared between two people.
    b. the food will not be cooked.
    c. a person's daily diet consists of two thousand calories.
    d. the product contains preservatives.
    e. the product is unspoiled.

53. In order to reduce the risk of spinal bifida in infants, food manufacturers have begun adding
    a. calcium.
    b. folic acid.
    c. iron.
    d. vitamin K.
    e. magnesium.

54. Which of the following events decreases metabolism?
    a. Rapid weight loss
    b. Increase in muscle mass
    c. Slow weight gain
    d. Moderate workout
    e. Rapid weight gain

55. An ovo-lacto-vegetarian is a person who eats
   a. Fruits, vegetables, and grains
   b. Fruits, vegetables, grains, and poultry
   c. Fruits, vegetables, grains, and dairy products
   d. Fruits, vegetables, grains, dairy products, and eggs
   e. Fruits, vegetables, grains, and eggs

56. Sodium and chloride are major minerals; every day a person should consume ___ of each.
   a. 100 milligrams
   b. 1 kilogram
   c. 10 milligrams
   d. 10 grams
   e. 1 gram

57. Which of the following vitamins is water-soluble?
   a. Vitamin D
   b. Vitamin E
   c. Vitamin K
   d. Vitamin A
   e. Vitamin C

58. What is one problem associated with the over-consumption of protein?
   a. Dehydration
   b. Increased muscle mass
   c. Strained liver and kidneys
   d. Heart palpitations
   e. Dandruff

59. Which kind of oil is NOT an unsaturated fat?
   a. Corn oil
   b. Olive oil
   c. Canola oil
   d. Palm oil
   e. Sunflower oil

60. The amount of energy required to raise the temperature of one gram of water by one degree Celsius is a(n)
   a. joule.
   b. calorie.
   c. ohm.
   d. microgram.
   e. watt.

61. A person who is 41 to 100% heavier than his or her ideal weight is
   a. mildly obese.
   b. osteoporotic.
   c. diabetic.
   d. moderately obese.
   e. severely obese.

62. Which of the following statements is true?
      I. Bulimia can lead to tooth decay.
      II. Anorexics tend to have a distorted self-image.
      III. Bulimia does not always include purging.
   a. I only
   b. II only
   c. III only
   d. I and II only
   e. I, II, and III

63. Which nutrient is not present in high levels in dairy products?
   a. Vitamin B-12
   b. Iron
   c. Protein
   d. Vitamin A
   e. Calcium

64. Which of the following vitamins is known to improve the body's ability to use phosphorus and calcium?
   a. Vitamin E
   b. Vitamin D
   c. Vitamin B-3
   d. Vitamin K
   e. Vitamin A

65. Which of the following statements about stain removal is true?
   a. Stained garments can be safely ironed.
   b. A fresh stain can be cleaned with bar soap.
   c. Milk stains should be treated with hot water.
   d. Regular clothing can be washed alongside clothing with chemical stains.
   e. Stained clothing should be cleaned within 24 hours.

66. Which fabrication method, typical of outerwear, involves stitching a liner fabric in between two outer fabrics?
   a. Knitting
   b. Stitch-through
   c. Quilting
   d. Tufting
   e. Weaving

67. What is the name for wool that has been spun into a fine yarn from parallel threads?
    a. Worsted
    b. Cashmere
    c. Angora
    d. Polyester
    e. Spandex

68. Fuzzy fibers that ball up and adhere to the outside of a garment are said to be
    a. fuzzing.
    b. snagging.
    c. breathing.
    d. pilling.
    e. creasing.

69. What does the word *carded* mean when it appears on a clothing label?
    a. The garment has been evaluated by a licensed inspector.
    b. The garment is made of short and thick cotton fibers.
    c. The garment was not created in a sweat shop.
    d. The garment only contains one type of fiber.
    e. The garment is resistant to wrinkles.

70. Which of the following garments would be the most resistant to wrinkles?
    a. Rayon jacket
    b. Cotton t-shirt
    c. Silk shirt
    d. Linen pants
    e. Wool pants

71. What is one common problem with silk clothing?
    a. It is easily damaged by the sun.
    b. It is very susceptible to abrasions.
    c. It has a tendency to wrinkle.
    d. It is very flammable.
    e. It is coarse.

72. The FTC does NOT mandate that clothing labels include
    a. the country of origin.
    b. whether the garment contains mink or rabbit.
    c. an indication of whether wool is new or recycled.
    d. the Registered Identification Number or name of the manufacturer.
    e. each fiber class represented in the item.

73. On which of the following fabrics is it safe to use bleach occasionally?
    a. Spandex
    b. Silk
    c. Cotton
    d. Wool
    e. Cashmere

74. Which fabric is best for blocking sunlight?
    a. Green satin
    b. Black cotton
    c. White cotton
    d. Black satin
    e. Red cotton

75. In interior design, the arrangement of elements in a pattern around some central point is known as
    a. symmetrical balance.
    b. gradation balance.
    c. asymmetrical balance.
    d. harmonic balance.
    e. radial balance.

76. In which layout pattern are spaces arranged along a linear path, with major elements at either end?
    a. Radial layout
    b. Dumbbell layout
    c. Clustered layout
    d. Doughnut layout
    e. Centralized layout

77. Which of the following represents the Fibonacci sequence?
    a. 0, 1, 1, 2, 3, 5...
    b. 0, 1, 2, 4, 8, 16...
    c. 0, 1, 1.5., 2, 2.5...
    d. 0, 1, 3, 6, 9, 12...
    e. 0, 2, 4, 6, 8, 10...

78. Which of the following is considered to be the most important determinant of human comfort in housing?
    a. Relative humidity
    b. Mean radiant temperature
    c. Air temperature
    d. Air quality
    e. Ventilation

79. Fabric hung across the window by a rod that covers either the extreme ends of the window or the entire window is called a
    a. curtain.
    b. louvered shutter.
    c. drapery.
    d. grille.
    e. Roman shade.

80. A kitchen is fourteen feet long and ten feet wide, but it has an adjoining pantry four feet deep and four feet wide. What is the gross area of the kitchen?
    a. 24 square feet
    b. 32 square feet
    c. 140 square feet
    d. 156 square feet
    e. 2240 square feet

81. The synthetic woodwork finish that creates the most durable surface is
    a. lacquer.
    b. polyurethane.
    c. varnish.
    d. vinyl.
    e. polyester.

82. Which of the following is NOT a good strategy for instructing a learning-disabled student?
    a. Breaking a complicated problem into simple steps
    b. Encouraging students to strive for perfection
    c. Establishing a daily routine
    d. Incorporating movement and tactile instruction whenever possible
    e. Delivering abstract concepts through dialogue with students

83. Which of the following is a cognitive objective of consumer science?
    a. Ability to select drapes
    b. Ability to arrange furniture
    c. Ability to load a shopping cart
    d. Ability to restrain consumer impulses
    e. Ability to create a personal budget

84. What is one common criticism of cooperative education programs?
    a. They isolate students from the rest of the academic community.
    b. They do not provide on-the-job training.
    c. They do not help students make career choices.
    d. They separate the business and academic communities.
    e. They decrease student motivation.

85. Which of the following is NOT one of the focuses of Junior Achievement programs at the high school level?
    a. Personal finance
    b. Business and entrepreneurship
    c. Community service
    d. Work preparation
    e. Economics

86. What is the primary focus of the FCCLA?
    a. College admission
    b. Academic achievement
    c. The family
    d. Career advancement
    e. Consumer education

87. A needs assessment for a family and consumer science program should begin with
    a. a gap analysis.
    b. lesson plans.
    c. prioritization.
    d. time management analysis.
    e. a survey of summative assessment results.

88. Which of the following is NOT a necessary component of an effective syllabus?
    a. Grading scale
    b. Mission statement
    c. List of community resources
    d. Clear assessment objectives
    e. Course content

89. A lesson plan calls for students to act out a negotiating scenario in which pairs of students try to settle a hypothetical dispute between a husband and wife over money. Which learning disability might prevent a student from succeeding at this task?
    a. Dyssemia
    b. Apraxia
    c. Dysgraphia
    d. Dyslexia
    e. Visual perception disorder

90. When evaluating Internet research, what is the least important consideration?
    a. Whether the website has an editorial board
    b. The organization that maintains the website
    c. The presence of links to similar websites
    d. The last time the website was updated
    e. An affiliation with the United States government

91. Many high-school students believe that the most important content area in family and consumer science is
    a. housing.
    b. the family.
    c. consumer science.
    d. personal finance.
    e. food and nutrition.

92. The original purpose of family and consumer science education was to
   a. redress social problems such as child labor and the repression of women.
   b. improve women's housekeeping skills.
   c. encourage frugality during the World War II.
   d. reinforce traditional family roles.
   e. encourage the use of household appliances.

93. Which of the following activities would best develop the psychomotor skills of elementary-school students?
   a. Learning to calculate compound interest
   b. Creating a budget for their school wardrobe
   c. Looking up banking terms in the dictionary
   d. Setting up a mock storefront for a retail business
   e. Drawing a picture of their ideal house

94. Name one advantage of large classes.
   a. Close relations between students and teacher
   b. Greater access to resources
   c. Expanded range of teaching methods
   d. Less record-keeping
   e. Greater comfort for the teacher

95. Which of the following is NOT a relevant factor when making changes in the family and consumer sciences curriculum?
   a. Experience
   b. Knowledge
   c. Time
   d. Skill
   e. Expense

96. A teacher is dividing the class up into groups for a project. What is the best way to avoid gender discrimination?
   a. Segregate the groups by gender.
   b. Encourage boys to include girls when making decisions.
   c. Encourage girls to handle tasks related to math.
   d. Be sure each group is comprised of both boys and girls.
   e. Give leadership positions to at least one boy and one girl in each group.

97. The primary determinant of whether a teacher will adopt instructional technology is
   a. estimated cost.
   b. student interest.
   c. perceived usefulness.
   d. the teacher's aptitude.
   e. geographic location.

98. The Carl D. Perkins Improvement Act of 2006 mandated that
    a. children with disabilities be given a free lunch.
    b. the curriculum of family and consumer science be aligned with general content standards.
    c. family and consumer science teachers obtain an undergraduate degree.
    d. students in family and consumer sciences pass a written examination.
    e. family and consumer sciences teachers focus on career training.

99. An activity that requires students to describe their ideal home falls within the
    a. psychomotor domain.
    b. analytic domain.
    c. cognitive domain.
    d. affective domain.
    e. synthetic domain.

100. Children between the ages of six and eight should be able to
    a. make change.
    b. compare the prices of products.
    c. maintain spending records.
    d. use the terminology associated with banking.
    e. count coins.

Answer Key and Explanations

1. B: Individuation is the process through which a person comes to think of himself or herself as a distinct person despite membership in a family. The development of children in a family can be seen as an ongoing process of individuation. Children at first identify entirely with the mores, norms, and values of their family; it is only after prolonged exposure to other people outside the home that a child will begin to question his or her upbringing and perhaps modify his or her belief system. A fully individualized person is able to maintain a coherent personality without necessarily renouncing membership in a family with which he or she may have some disagreement.

2. D: People who live in an agrarian society are more likely to live with their extended family. An extended family is comprised of more than one adult couple. For instance, it might include a man and a woman, their children, and their grandchildren. Agrarian societies in which people tend the same land for their entire lives are more conducive to the maintenance of the extended family. This is in part because it is more difficult for a large group to move around together. In modern, industrial, urban, and nomadic societies, it is more common for people to be grouped together in nuclear families. A nuclear family includes one adult couple and their children.

3. D: Financial stability is not one of the factors necessary for a person to commit emotionally to a marriage. This fact is interesting, since money is one of the main issues leading many divorces. However, many experts agree that it is much more important for partners to have good self-esteem, empathy, a feeling of permanence in the relationship, and strong personal identities. Solid marriages weather the inevitable hard times with a mixture of humor, empathy, and habit. The idea of empathy is particularly important in marriage because it implies that each partner may not fully understand the other. Nevertheless, a loving spouse will try to help whenever possible.

4. A: Having a young child has no measurable effect on job satisfaction. Curiously, this is true for both men and women. Research suggests that parents often feel some strain as they occupy multiple roles, but this is offset by the enjoyment they derive from their work. Having a newborn, on the other hand, has a noticeably damaging effect on job satisfaction. The demands of caring for a newborn, as well as the desire to spend as much time as possible with this new child, make it unpleasant to be away from home for any reason. Flexible scheduling, high wages, and intellectual challenge are all directly correlated with job satisfaction.

5. C: After divorce, the first step a person should take is to accept that the divorce is final and the marriage is over. This is easier said than done, as psychologists estimate that it takes most people at least two years to accept divorce entirely. Until this is reached, the divorcee should not initiate a new relationship. The best way to complete the process of acceptance is to establish an individual identity. This may include developing a balance between being single and being a parent. It is appropriate to plan for the future, but people should be aware that it is impossible to predict what they will want once they have fully processed the finality of the divorce.

6. D: Of the given pairs, sibling rivalry would likely be greatest for brothers aged 3 and 5. In general, sibling rivalry is most pronounced in same-sex siblings within three years of age. In the first eight to ten years of life, siblings tend to alternate between cooperation and competition. As they grow older, they will often spend little time together for a few years, but during adolescence will gradually develop empathy for one another. Most research suggests that adult relationships between siblings simply exaggerate the tone of the relationship of youth; that is, good relationships get better and bad relationships get worse.

7. B: Married women typically earn a lower wage than single women. This is an exception to the general trend, which is that married people are healthier, wealthier, and more content than their single counterparts. Married men are less likely to abuse alcohol and drugs, and less likely to become depressed. Married women are healthier and more likely to report satisfaction with their home lives. One reason why married women may earn less money is that they are more likely to be raising children, and therefore less focused on professional development. Despite reports about the decline of marriage, an overwhelming majority of Americans will marry at least once during their lives.

8. E: In general, accepting a stepparent is hardest for adolescent girls. Of course, this process is not easy for sons and daughters of any age. However, research suggests that the bond between a stepparent, in particular a stepfather, and an adolescent girl takes the longest to form. One possible reason for this phenomenon is that stepfathers tend to be less engaged with stepdaughters than with stepsons. The effect of remarriage on children is much the same as divorce because it involves a fundamental restructuring of the family concept. Nevertheless, stepparents who work to engage with their stepchildren can develop positive relationships over time.

9. A: Both the content and the style of family communication are important. For instance, a parent may deliver a positive message and then undermine it by demonstrating contrary behavior. The members of a family should work on communicating positively. The other answer choices are true statements about families. The decisions made by families tend to reinforce the status quo in the interest of conformity and conflict avoidance. For reasons both genetic and environmental, the members of families are likely to struggle with the same sorts of problems in life. Despite a general tendency toward stability and consistency, families inevitably change in response to the aging of each member and to pressures from the environment. Finally, it is a central tenet of family science that it is impossible to understand a family member without understanding the family as a whole.

10. D: According to John Gottman, the best response to criticism by a spouse is humor. Gottman has performed extensive research on the interactions between married couples and has identified characteristics of both durability and divorce. When the criticized partner responds to criticism by deflecting or soothing the other person, tempers are quelled and the partnership remains strong. Gottman's research suggests that there is a classic pattern of degenerating communication in an unsuccessful relationship. The pattern begins with criticism that is not directed at a certain behavior, but at the other person as a whole. In other words, the criticism of unsuccessful couples tends to lean toward character assassination. Eventually, these negative interactions lead to contempt, in which one partner openly disparages and disrespects the other. The inevitable response to contempt is

defensiveness, followed by stonewalling, or a total lack of communication. When couples stop communicating, the relationship is not likely to endure.

11. B: The greatest amount of variation between people of the same age is found during early adolescence. The onset of puberty may occur at any time over the span of five years, though it typically occurs earlier in females than in males. The changes brought on by puberty are monumental and can cause rapid changes in personality, physical development, and emotional maturity. Teachers need to be aware of these changes, particularly when working with middle-school children. Family and consumer science teachers may need to act as liaisons between parents and their children, as family relationships can become strained during early adolescence.

12. A: When two children have a dispute and agree to settle it according to their mother's opinion, they are engaging in arbitration. In arbitration, two conflicting parties agree to rely on the advice of a supposedly impartial third party. Sometimes, the parties will also establish guidelines for the way a decision is to be reached. In parenting, it can be difficult to settle a dispute with arbitration, since children are unlikely to honor a decision that goes against their interests. Conciliation is a method of settling disputes in which the conflicting parties are simply asked to meet and converse, with the idea that a resolution will naturally occur as a result of this meeting. In mediation, the conflicting parties decide to enlist the aid of an impartial third party as they attempt to settle their differences. The parties in mediation do not agree to follow the advice of the third party. In negotiation, two parties try to agree on terms that are acceptable to both. Negotiation in family life is a bit like compromise. Finally, restorative justice is a system in which the person who has been wronged gets some kind of compensation from the wrongdoer. When parents force one sibling to apologize to the other, they are essentially using restorative justice.

13. C: In general, the children of working mothers have greater self-esteem. There is no one reason for this phenomenon, although one can speculate that girls might be inspired by the positive example of a successful working mother. The other answer choices are incorrect statements about working mothers. The daughters of working mothers tend to be more independent, and they are likely to have a more egalitarian view of gender relations. When the sons of working mothers are unsupervised, their performance in school tends to decline. It is very important for both parents to have a positive attitude about maternal employment, and it is especially important for husbands to support their wives in ways that can be perceived positively by children.

14. C: Structured family therapists assume that during times of conflict, family members will take sides to consolidate power. Although this process is natural, it can become problematic if the groups last for too long or create a permanent imbalance of power. A structured family therapist surveys problematic family coalitions and destabilizes them. The idea that family life is a series of actions and reactions is an assumption of Milan systemic family therapy. This approach to family therapy emphasizes patterns of behavior that lock family members into their roles, therefore inhibiting their personal growth. Behavioral family therapists assume that bad behavior persists when it is reinforced. These therapists strive to show family members how they may be inadvertently rewarding the very behavior they seek to discourage. Finally, object relations family therapists assume that ill will in a family is often a result of negative projection. In other words, the members of a family may attribute their own negative characteristics to their family members.

- 98 -

15. D: One drawback of inpatient treatment for alcoholism is that it is expensive. In addition, inpatient programs are often not covered by health insurance, so the patient and his or her family may be forced to pay out of pocket. The efficacy of these programs is well established, however. Some studies estimate that 70% of the participants in inpatient programs stay sober for at least five years. Many of these inpatient programs include the twelve-step process, most famously represented by Alcoholics Anonymous. Patients cannot continue to drink while they are enrolled in an inpatient program, since they are living on the grounds of the treatment facility. Finally, it is true that inpatient programs require the personal commitment of the patient, but this is true of all rehabilitation programs.

16. D: According to Piaget, the ability to imagine the mental lives of others emerges during the preoperational stage. This is the second of the four stages outlined by Piaget and typically occurs between the ages of 2 and 7. The ability to imaginatively construct the mental life of another person is called sympathy. The first stage in the Piaget model is sensorimotor, which lasts from birth until about age 2. During this time, the sense organs become activated, and the child learns about object permanence (that is, objects continue to exist even when they leave the perceptual field). In the third stage, known as concrete operational, the child improves his or her cognition and realizes that objects with different shapes may have the same volume. This stage occurs between the ages of 7 and 12. In the formal operational stage, the capacity for abstract thought is developed. When this stage occurs (and it does not occur for every person), it typically occurs after age 12. Primary socialization is not one of Piaget's stages; it is a person's first experience of living among other people. Typically, a person undergoes primary socialization within his or her family.

17. B: One example of role strain is a new teacher who struggles to maintain authority in the classroom. Role strain is any hardship a person encounters while trying to fulfill the socially accepted requirements of a role. Individuals are almost never a perfect fit for any role they attempt to inhabit, so role strain is inevitable. A public speaker who cultivates his or her expertise is displaying role performance, or the conscious fulfillment of a social role's characteristics. A person whose parents die goes through the role exit process, because he or she no longer is in the role of a son or daughter. A child who imagines what it would be like to be a police officer is demonstrating role taking, in which a person imagines what it would be like to fill a certain social role. Finally, a substitute teacher who waits tables on the weekend exemplifies the idea of the role set, or the different roles that a single person can inhabit at a given point in his or her life.

18. E: An eight year-old with the mental age of a ten year-old has an IQ (intelligence quotient) of 125. IQ is measured by dividing mental age by actual age and then multiplying the quotient. Mental age is defined as the average amount of knowledge held by a person at a given age. Of course, this is a rather arbitrary figure, dependent on the prevailing norms of education. For this reason, IQ is seen as a somewhat unreliable indicator of intellectual development. Many critics feel that it ignores intuitive, spatial, and creative abilities. The average IQ should be 100, since this is the score a person will receive when their mental age is the same as their actual age.

19. D: The student is in the contemplation stage of the transtheoretical model of change. In this stage, a person recognizes the need for a change but is not yet prepared to take action.

This is the second of six stages. In the first stage, precontemplation, the person does not yet recognize that he or she has a problem. In the third stage, preparation/commitment, the person determines that a change is necessary and begins to collect information about solutions. The fourth stage is action, when the person begins to change his or her behavior. In the fifth stage, maintenance, the person notes the benefits of the new behavior and strives to avoid falling back into bad habits. In the sixth and final stage, termination, the person has made the new behavior habitual and is very unlikely to backslide.

20. E: Echolalia is an infant's nonsensical imitation of adult speech. Most children begin exhibiting echolalia at about nine months of age. This is one of the steps in language acquisition. There are six such stages: crying, cooing, babbling, echolalia, holophrastic speech, and telegraphic speech. Over the first few months of life, an infant will develop different cries to express different emotions. After six or eight weeks, the infant will begin to display a vowel-intensive warbling sound, known as cooing. Babies between four and six months old typically begin to make a babbling noise, which over time will come to resemble the baby's native language. Echolalia is the next step, followed by holophrastic speech, in which the baby uses single words to communicate more complex ideas. Finally, between eighteen and twenty-four months, the child will initiate telegraphic speech, combinations of words that make sense together. Deep structuring is not one of the steps of language acquisition. The linguist Noam Chomsky posited that language includes a surface structure (parts of speech, vocabulary, e.g.) and a deep structure (underlying meanings of words).

21. A: The major criticism of Levinson's "seasons" of life model is that it overstates the importance of the mid-life crisis. Levinson outlined four major periods of life: infancy to adolescence; early adulthood; middle adulthood; and late adulthood. The major crisis of life according to Levinson was the realization during middle adulthood that the dreams established in early adulthood are not entirely attainable. This brings on the mid-life crisis. Subsequent psychology has indicated that this crisis does not occur for all people and is often not very severe when it does occur. However, Levinson's model does acknowledge the suffering of life and does address the last years of life, in which a person confronts and reconciles with mortality. Levinson also asserts that life transitions are made consciously and with a great deal of stress. Finally, Levinson emphasizes the role of parents in shaping the early years and thus the foundation of a person's personality development.

22. A: Sudden interest in a new hobby is not a warning sign of teen depression. Teenagers at risk of depression tend to withdraw and will not be likely to take on a new hobby. Instead, depressed teenagers lose interest in activities that previously engaged and pleased them. The other four answer choices are common warning signs of teen depression. Depression is also thought to be hereditary, so teenagers with a family history of the illness should be especially alert to these signs.

23. B: The different treatment given to students who excel in math as opposed to those who excel in English is known as horizontal socialization. Horizontal socialization is a fundamental difference in the treatment of people who inhabit different roles. Doctors and teachers, for instance, are treated differently by society, even though one profession is not necessarily prized more than the other. Vertical socialization, on the other hand, is the different treatment individuals receive when they occupy different class positions. Wealthy people, for example, are socialized differently than poor people. Resocialization is the

intentional adjustment of a person's socialization, typically in the hope that the person will become better integrated into society. People who are released from prison, for instance, must be resocialized into society. Anticipatory socialization occurs when a person expects to enter a new role in the future and adjusts his or her behavior accordingly. At the end of summer vacation, for example, students might start to adjust their clothing and hygiene as they look forward to the start of the school year. Desocialization is the relinquishing of a previously-held role. In a sense, all people are involved in a constant process of desocialization, since they are constantly casting off roles and taking on new ones.

24. D: Thrift is not one of the areas of emotional intelligence. There are five such areas: self-awareness, empathy, personal motivation, altruism, and the ability to love and be loved. These areas were outlined by the psychologist Daniel Goleman, who was one of the first experts to suggest that IQ is an insufficient measure of a person. The development of emotional intelligence is also important. It is possible to improve emotional intelligence by cultivating self-expression and learning to listen to one's conscience.

25. A: The United States actually has a higher rate of teen pregnancy than many other developed countries. However, this rate has decreased over the past twenty years, due to effective instruction and the distribution of birth control. Nevertheless, the rate of teen pregnancy remains too high, especially among Hispanics and African-Americans. Because teen pregnancy has such a damaging effect on success in life, family and consumer science teachers are encouraged to treat this subject in their discussion of family life. The Center for Disease Control offers a number of resources related to teen pregnancy.

26. A: An effective time management plan will encourage students to do the most difficult tasks first. This is considered by time management advisors to be the single most important aspect of successful time management, which is increasingly important in an age of information overload and nonstop distraction. This last point is the reason why answer choice B is incorrect: There is no way to eliminate every possible distraction. Instead, an effective time management plan should try to mitigate the damage of inevitable distractions. It is not necessary for a time management plan to be so comprehensive as to include meals, though some students may find it useful to do so. Making lists is the cornerstone of time management, since lists help students to prioritize their tasks and keep from feeling overwhelmed by the many things they have to do. Finally, because a time management plan will be tailored to the life of the individual, it will be different for each student.

27. C: When a daily routine has been established, it is less necessary to create a list of things to do. Making lists is one of the best ways to organize tasks and to keep from being overwhelmed by responsibilities. However, a daily routine makes certain tasks habitual, which can eventually eliminate the need for the list. For instance, a parent might get up every morning and go through the same steps to get his children ready for school. Since this set of tasks is performed habitually, it does not need to be written down. In addition, the development of a routine helps get the body and mind accustomed to performing certain tasks at certain times. Most people find that a routine makes it less difficult for them to find the motivation to perform unpleasant tasks.

28. D: In the system outlined by Hersey and Blanchard, the leadership style that emphasizes the performance of tasks and ignores the development of positive relationships is called telling. Hersey and Blanchard's model, known as situational leadership, describes four different leadership styles: telling, delegating, selling, and participating. These styles are distinguished by the degree to which they emphasize either task performance or relationship building. The delegating style entails little commitment to either function. A delegating leader passes off authority to his or her subordinates. A selling leader is heavily involved with both task performance and the building of relationships. Such a leader is constantly engaged with his or her subordinates, helping them do their jobs and keeping them motivated. While a telling leader is very involved in the performance of tasks, he or she is not very interested in building positive relationships with subordinates. Such a leader is likely to micromanage subordinates, often to their annoyance. A participating leader is not involved in tasks but is very invested in his or her relationships with subordinates. Such a leader rarely asserts authority over the other members of the group.

29. D: Most of the time, the best way for a family to decide on a vacation destination is to have a discussion and then have the final decision made by the parents. It is important for parents to give their children a sense of involvement in the process, though the parents should retain the ultimate decision. When parents make decisions without consulting their children, the children are less likely to be willing to participate fully. On the other hand, when children are included in making important decisions, they often are governed by emotion or whim rather than reason. The best decision-making system, then, is a combination of discussion and parental leadership.

30. E: Of the given options, the best way to limit a child's television time is to set a timer and turn the television off when the alarm sounds. This strategy has a number of advantages. It establishes ahead of time the amount of television that can be watched, so the child will not be surprised or feel that the discipline is arbitrary. Setting up a timer also creates an objective method of enforcement with which the child cannot argue or attempt to negotiate. In this, as in many cases, it is helpful to create firm, consistent rules that the child can understand. When boundaries are consistent, the child will quickly learn the futility of arguing and will more easily come to accept the limitations on his or her desire. Scaring the child or using other negative reinforcement is a less desirable solution. Merely suggesting that the child go outside is unlikely to be influential unless it is backed up by other methods.

31. B: Group polarization is a phenomenon in which a group makes more extreme decisions than any member would make independently. Management experts believe that this is due to the desire for conformity and the subsequent reinforcement of whatever solutions are first suggested. Rather than critique another group member and create disharmony, participants will often go along and even amplify the first opinion given. Organizational conflict can actually be a healthy thing, since it indicates that views are being aired openly. Social facilitation is a phenomenon in which the presence of others encourages a person to work harder. Groupthink is similar to group polarization, except that it does not necessarily result in extreme decisions. Groupthink is the suppression of reason in the interest of maintaining group cohesion. Social loafing is a phenomenon in which people do not work as hard in a group, often because they feel their contributions will not be respected.

32. B: Members of a family are more likely to be motivated when their goal is well defined. For instance, if parents decide to save for a new car, their children will be more likely to accept material sacrifices once they know about the underlying goal of these sacrifices. People in general have a hard time accepting changes or commands when there is no communicated rationale. In addition, motivation toward a family goal tends to be higher when members volunteer their participation. A tangible reward that seems fair is another way motivation is increased. Also, the members of a family are better able to stay motivated when they can objectively evaluate their own performance and then use this evaluation to make corrections. Finally, motivation cannot remain high when some members of the family feel that they are working much harder than other members.

33. C: Research has shown that a compressed workweek increases employee satisfaction. The normal work week consists of 5 eight-hour days; a compressed schedule increases the amount of work time for each day but decreases the number of days. Typically, the total amount of time spent at work stays the same. For instance, a common compressed workweek consists of 4 ten-hour days. There is not any demonstrated correlation between a compressed workweek and employee performance. However, employees who have a long commute are generally very enthusiastic about such a plan, since it eliminates one commute to and from the office. This advantage would be irrelevant to employees who work from home.

34. A: The first step towards eliminating wasted time is to keep a log of how time is spent. In the chaotic modern world, almost everyone feels as if he or she is moving in a dozen different directions at once. The natural result is the creeping suspicion that time is being wasted and maximum productivity is not being achieved. Time management experts agree that the first step in eliminating wasted time is to determine where it is being wasted. This is done by keeping an activity log for several days and then studying it to find where time is typically wasted. Once the time wasters have been identified, it will become easier to tighten up the daily schedule.

35. D: A five year-old is probably too young to mop the kitchen floor. Mopping requires a degree of upper-body strength that a child of this age is unlikely to possess. However, a five year-old should be able to complete all of the other tasks listed as answer choices. Moreover, children at this age are often very enthusiastic about helping with household chores, particularly if they are given a chance to work independently. At this age, children are interested in participating in adult activities whenever possible, and parents should take advantage of this interest.

36. A: The proper decision-making process begins by defining the problem to be solved. Too often, students start working on potential solutions before the problem has been fully articulated. This leads to half-measures and ineffective decisions. Only after the problem has been outlined in its entirety should possible solutions be considered. It is a good idea to write down these options. Whenever possible, the emphasis should be on long-term solutions rather than quick fixes. In some cases, it may be determined that there is not enough information to make an informed decision. If this is the case, either information should be collected or, if this is impossible, the decision maker should figure out a strategy for mitigating this problem.

37. D: When making a schedule, children should be encouraged to both include some free time and place the hardest tasks first. However, children should not be encouraged to block out long stretches for completing all homework because this would be too vague. One of the hallmarks of an effective schedule is specificity, so large categories like homework should be broken down into smaller tasks. At the least, the child should divide homework into subjects, and it may even be necessary to subdivide subjects into particular tasks. It is important, however, for a schedule to include some free time because interruptions and distractions are inevitable. If a schedule is too rigid, the student is likely to become discouraged when he or she is unable to meet it. Also, it is a good idea to place the hardest tasks first, since the student will have the highest energy and mental resources then.

38. B: Drop-in child care is useful when the regular childcare provider is unavailable. Drop-in child care is a service offered by some daycares and other child care centers. When parents have a specific need for childcare, when their normal provider is closed, for instance, they can call the drop-in center and see if there is any room for their child. The parents will need to have registered with the drop-in center ahead of time. This arrangement helps child care facilities operate at maximum capacity and helps parents fill unexpected holes in their child care schedule. Drop-in child care can be expensive, however, and may not be a valid option for children with special needs. Whether a child is in school or not would have little bearing on the utility of drop-in child care.

39. D: One disadvantage of dealing with consumer finance companies is that they often charge high interest rates. Consumer finance companies lend money to private citizens who want to make a purchase. There are few lending restrictions related to the purpose of the loan. Because these loans are considered to be risky, consumer finance companies often charge exorbitant interest rates. In most cases, however, they will accept property as security. The high interest rates and predatory business practices associated with consumer finance companies should dissuade consumers from dealing with them unless absolutely necessary. Before entering into an agreement with a consumer finance company, one should consider whether the planned purchase is absolutely necessary.

40. E: Restaurants are the most common employer of high-school students. This assertion is based on data from the United States Bureau of Labor Statistics. The presence of so many students in food service jobs can be useful to both the family and the consumer science teacher. These students will have direct experience with the cost of food, as well as with the nutritional choices available in a restaurant. It is an excellent idea to allow students to incorporate their work experience into classroom activities.

41. A: Borrowers with a poor credit rating will not be eligible for a bank's prime rate. The prime rate is the lowest rate of interest offered by a commercial bank or other lending institution. It is made available only to borrowers with pristine credit ratings, since these people and businesses are most likely to repay the loan according to the agreed-upon schedule. Savings deposits, demand deposits, and certificates of deposit are all investitures made by the consumer in a bank, and therefore do not depend on credit rating. A savings deposit can be withdrawn at any time, while a certificate of deposit must be kept in the bank for a prescribed length of time. A demand deposit is essentially the same thing as a checking account, because the funds within it can be withdrawn at any time and in any amount.

Banks are required to have deposit insurance to guarantee that they will be able to return the funds invested by customers.

42. E: Research suggests that children in daycare are better at articulating their desires. It is believed that this ability develops because the child is dealing with a caregiver who, unlike the child's parent, may not intuit demands. The other answer choices are false statements. Research shows that children in daycare are more likely to be aggressive and disobedient, perhaps because they feel the need to advocate their own interests away from home. Doctors emphasize the importance of establishing the parent-child bond before starting daycare. Children in daycare make friends more easily, perhaps because they get more practice at interacting with others. The value of daycare is closely correlated with the quality of the supervision.

43. B: Presidents Kennedy and Nixon did not include the right to affordability among the consumer rights asserted during the 1960s. Businesses do not have any obligation to sell products at prices within reach of the average consumer. There were five essential consumer rights promulgated at that time: the right to a safe product; the right to redress; the right to be heard; the right to be informed; and the right to choose. The government enforces laws that require businesses to sell safe products or to clearly warn consumers about products that are not always safe. The right to redress enables consumers to receive a refund or compensation of some kind when a product does them harm. Consumers have a right to speak and be acknowledged by businesses. Consumers also have a right to as much information about products as they desire. Finally, consumers have a right to choose among a variety of products; it is with this in mind that the government enforces laws against monopoly.

44. D: It is generally agreed that a family should spend no more than 25% of its income on housing. Although some lenders are willing to give money to homebuyers who will spend up to 40% of their income on housing, this is considered a risky loan. Such a loan is especially risky when the borrower has other long-term debt besides housing costs. As a consumer, it is wise to create a detailed budget before committing any funds to housing costs.

45. C: Purchasing a DVD is a discretionary expense because it is based on personal desire rather than need. In other words, it is an expense made at the discretion of the consumer. Discretionary expenses are those over which a consumer has the most control. A comprehensive budget must include discretionary expenses as well as fixed and variable expenses. Fixed expenses, such as rent, are the same every month. Variable expenses, including groceries, school supplies, and heating oil, are always present but vary in amount over the course of a year.

46. C: For most people, it makes sense to set up a personal budget on a monthly basis. Expenses such as rent and bills tend to be due on a monthly basis, and a month is long enough that brief fluctuations in food costs will balance out. Of course, a person needs to be sensitive to the fact that some months will be more expensive than others. For instance, if a person lives in a cold climate, he or she is likely to spend more money on heating during the winter months. Those who get paid every week or every two weeks will need to make a simple calculation to determine their monthly earnings.

47. B: If Denise has a credit card with an APR of 4.5% and she maintains an average balance of $2500 throughout the year, the account will accrue $112.50 in interest. APR stands for annual percentage rate; it is the amount of interest charged over the course of twelve months. To calculate the amount of interest accruing on Denise's account, multiply her average balance by the APR (making sure to convert 4.5% into the decimal 0.045). The product of this calculation is the amount of interest accrued on the account over the course of a year.

48. D: It is not a good idea to visit fewer than three daycare providers before selecting one. Each of these visits should be thorough and should include a full tour and an extensive conversation with the care providers. Beforehand, a parent or guardian should make a list of questions for the meeting. For instance, one should get a description of a typical day at the facility, as well as spend some time observing the childcare providers at work. Whenever possible, children should visit the daycare facility before starting to go there regularly. Toilet training is handled differently by different provides, so if this is an issue, parents should inquire about the institutional policy. Children should be allowed to bring a favorite toy, blanket, or stuffed animal to daycare. Parents or guardians, especially those for whom this is the first daycare experience, should visit at least three daycare facilities before making a decision. Finally, parents or guardians should try to discuss going to daycare with their child in a positive manner as early as possible.

49. E: A debenture bond is secured only by the assets and earnings of the corporation that issues it. This is just one kind of bond sold by corporations to raise money. Consumers should be apprised of the various types of bonds offered so that they can make wise investment decisions. The general difference between bonds is the security offered; that is, the way in which the corporation guarantees repayment. A collateral trust bond uses the stocks and bonds of other companies as collateral. A mortgage bond is secured by a piece of mortgaged property, such as an office building or factory. A sinking-fund bond is a form of debenture bond in which the corporation additionally pledges to pay back the money slowly over a long time. A convertible bond can be traded in for common stock at any time.

50. D: The major benefit of vitamin A is that it helps the body produce healthy hair and skin. Carrots, pumpkins, fish, and eggs are all good sources of vitamin A. Help with forming new cells is a major benefit of folate, or folic acid. There is a great deal of folate in spinach and fortified grains. Vitamin C is one of the primary disease-fighting nutrients. It is obtained most effectively from citrus fruits and broccoli. Concentration and alertness are improved by vitamin B-12. It is most abundant in fish, poultry, and eggs. Calcium is a mineral that helps muscles contract. It is abundant in dairy products and sardines.

51. A: The United States Department of Agriculture recommends between six and eleven servings of bread, cereal, rice, and pasta daily. This is the most recommended servings of all the food groups. The other recommended serving amounts are as follows: vegetables (three to five servings); fruits (two to four servings); milk, yogurt, and cheese (two to three servings); meat, poultry, fish, eggs, dry beans, and nuts (two to three servings); and fats, oils, and sweets (less than a serving).

52. C: The recommended daily values listed on food packaging assume a daily diet of two thousand calories. Adult males are generally advised to eat about this many calories every day. Women and children, however, may require fewer calories, while athletes may require more. When one's recommended caloric intake is considerably lower or higher than two thousand, one must make necessary adjustments to the daily values.

53. B: Food manufacturers now add folic acid to their products because it has been shown to reduce the risk of spinal bifida in infants. Folic acid is a B vitamin that aids in the synthesis of hemoglobin, which is required to transport oxygen throughout the bloodstream. Pregnant women, women who are trying to become pregnant, and elderly people should all ensure that their diet includes foods with folic acid. There are also a number of safe supplements containing folic acid.

54. A: Losing weight quickly decreases the metabolism. Nutritionists and doctors believe that this is a form of self-defense by the body, which senses that food is not as available and therefore tries to limit its use of calories. All of the other answer choices are events that increase metabolism. Weight gain always raises metabolism, in part because there is more muscle or fat to provide with nutrients. Muscle burns more calories than fat, so an increase in muscle mass will correlate with an increase in metabolism. Any exercise tends to increase metabolism.

55. D: An ovo-lacto-vegetarian is a person who eats fruits, vegetables, grains, dairy products, and eggs. These people get most of their proteins from beans, eggs, milk, and cheese. There are several other kinds of vegetarians. A vegan is someone who eats only plant foods; vegans do not eat any meat or animal product, including honey. Lacto-vegetarians eat fruits, vegetables, grains, and dairy products.

56. A: A person should consume 100 milligrams of major minerals, including sodium and chloride, every day. Of course, sodium and chloride can both be obtained from table salt. Some of the other major minerals are potassium, calcium, phosphorus, and magnesium. Trace minerals, such as iron, zinc, and copper, need only be consumed at a rate of 10 milligrams every day. The precise effect of these minerals on the body has not yet been determined.

57. E: Vitamin C is water-soluble, meaning that it is absorbed into the blood stream and can be forced out of the body through urine and sweat. For example, caffeinated beverages can increase the urine stream and thereby diminish the absorption of water-soluble nutrients like vitamin C. Vitamin B is another water-soluble nutrient. Other vitamins, including A, D, E, and K, are absorbed by the intestinal membrane; these vitamins are said to be fat-soluble. Vitamin D can also be obtained from sunlight.

58. C: An overconsumption of protein can put strain on the kidneys and liver. This is one reason why doctors discourage the use of body-building supplements and protein shakes unless under medical supervision. An excessive consumption of protein can lead to general imbalances in diet, which can undermine fitness in the long run. Protein does contribute to the development of muscle mass, but this is not necessarily a problem. Weight-lifting and vigorous physical activities require complex carbohydrates as well as proteins.

59. D: Palm oil is not an unsaturated fat. On the contrary, it is a saturated fat, meaning that excessive consumption of it can lead to heart disease. Coconut oil, butter, and lard are some of the other saturated fats. The other answer choices are unsaturated fats, which are better for the body. In fact, olive oil and canola oil can reduce the amount of cholesterol in the body.

60. B: A calorie is the amount of energy required to raise the temperature of one gram of water by one degree Celsius. In the United States, every packaged food must contain a listing of the number of calories per serving. Also, whereas in the past it was possible for manufacturers to confuse the consumer by indicating odd serving sizes, the designation of serving size is now regulated by the federal government. All the manufacturers of a particular product are required to use similar serving sizes.

61. D: A person who is 41 to 100% heavier than his or her ideal weight is moderately obese. Health professionals have divided obesity into three degrees: mild, moderate, and severe. A person who is less than 20% heavier than his or her ideal weight is considered merely overweight, but a person who is 20 to 40% heavier is considered mildly obese. People who are more than 100% heavier than their ideal weight are severely obese. Moderately obese people are much more likely to have diabetes or osteoporosis, but do not necessarily suffer from these conditions.

62. E: All three of the statements are true. Bulimia can lead to tooth decay, due to a combination of malnutrition and corrosion by stomach acid. Anorexics often have a distorted self-image, believing themselves to be much heavier than they actually are. Finally, bulimia does not always include purging (induced vomiting or defecation). Bulimics may obsessively exercise or abstain from food in order to lose weight. Both anorexia and bulimia are extremely dangerous and should be discussed at great length in the nutrition component of a family and consumer science class. These conditions are especially common among middle-school and high-school students.

63. B: Dairy products do not contain significant amounts of iron. The other answer choices, however, are nutrients that are abundant in dairy products. Riboflavin is another nutrient found in great quantities in dairy products. According to the USDA, people should eat two or three servings of dairy every day. A serving is equivalent to eight ounces of milk, a cup of yogurt, or one and a half ounces of cheese. People should be careful about which dairy products they consume, as many contain a great deal of fat.

64. B: Vitamin D is known to help the body absorb the phosphorus and calcium obtained through a person's diet. It is present in small amounts in foods like fish and eggs and is especially present in cod liver oil. Vitamin E is a major antioxidant, meaning that it eliminates cells that can have a deleterious effect on the body. This vitamin is found in good amounts in wheat germ oil, milk, and plant leaves. Vitamin B-3, also known as niacin, helps to reduce levels of cholesterol in the blood. It is found in yeast, dairy products, and wheat germ. Vitamin K promotes blood clotting. It is abundant in spinach, cabbage, and soybeans. Vitamin A contributes to the growth and maintenance of body tissues. It is particularly present in eggs, spinach, and liver.

65. E: Stained clothing should be cleaned within 24 hours; after a day, many stains will have set and will be almost impossible to remove. The other answer choices are false statements about stain removal. It is not a good idea to iron stained objects, as the heat is likely to set the stain. Bar soap should not be used on fresh stains, because it too has the capacity to set stains. Hot water can set stains caused by proteins, like blood, milk, and egg. It is not considered safe to wash clothing with chemical stains alongside regular laundry. Although most washing machines are strong enough to remove toxic chemicals, there is no sense in taking the risk.

66. C: Quilting is the fabrication method of stitching a liner fabric in between two outer fabrics. Because this process essentially creates a three-layered fabric, it is used in outerwear and clothing that is meant for cold weather. Knitting is the use of hooked needles to loop yarn threads together. Fabrics made by knitting tend to be very flexible. In stitch-through, a web of fiber is stitched together by a chain of smaller stitches. This technique is also known as malimo. Tufting is a process in which a woven backing has yarns inserted into it, where they are sealed in place with glue. This process, commonly used in the manufacture of carpets, is occasionally used in apparel as well. Finally, weaving is the creation of a network of three yarns, interconnected at right angles throughout the fabric.

67. A: Wool that has been combed into parallel threads and then spun into a fine yarn is known as worsted. Renowned for its strength, worsted is used in dresses and suits. Cashmere is an especially soft form of wool that is created from the hair of a specific Indian goat. Angora is another high-end wool made from the long hairs of the angora rabbit. Polyester is a synthetic textile, meaning that it is not made from plants or animals. It is often blended with other fibers in the creation of clothing. Spandex is a synthetic textile with amazing flexibility.

68. D: When the fuzzy fibers of a fabric ball up and adhere to the outside of the garment, they are said to be pilling. The degree to which a fabric "pills" is one criteria of durability. Fuzzing is the emergence of tiny fibers from a yarn, creating the effect of roughness on the outside of the garment. Snagging occurs when fibers catch and are pulled out of the weave. Breathing is the ability of a loosely woven fabric to allow the passage of air. Light fabrics tend to be better at breathing. Creasing is the creation of permanent folds in the fabric. Oftentimes, pants will be worn with an intentional crease along the front and back of the legs.

69. B: When it appears on a clothing label, the word *carded* means that the garment was made from short, thick cotton fibers. The use of carded fibers creates a fabric that is soft and strong. When the garment is made of long, straight cotton fibers, it is said to be combed. A combed fabric is smoother and shinier. A garment that only contains one type of fiber is considered pure. Garments that have been subjected to a permanent or durable press are more resistant to wrinkles. These processes are usually noted on the clothing label. A label may also indicate whether a garment has been inspected and that it was not created in a sweat shop.

70. E: Of the given garments, a pair of wool pants would be the most resistant to wrinkles. Because of the thickness of the fiber and the general looseness of the weave, clothing made of wool tends to be very resistant to wrinkles. This is one reason why wool clothing is so

useful for travel; it can be packed in a suitcase and not need to be ironed later. Silk and cotton products are moderately resistant to wrinkles. If packed properly, they can be worn without needing to be ironed. Rayon and linen are notoriously prone to wrinkles. Clothing made of these materials must be washed, dried, and stored properly.

71. A: One common problem with silk clothing is that it is easily damaged by the sun. Silken garments can fade quickly if they are not kept out of direct sunlight. For this reason, silk should be kept in a drawer or dark closet. The other answer choices are false statements. Silk is very resistant to abrasions and wrinkles, and it burns very slowly. Silk is renowned for its smoothness. It is considered one of the least coarse fabrics in the world.

72. B: The FTC does not mandate that clothing labels indicate whether the garment contains mink or rabbit. These fibers are considered to be specialty wools; therefore, they do not need to be identified by anything other than the word "wool" on the label. Fur labels, on the other hand, must declare the animal species and country of origin on the label. All of the other answer choices are pieces of information that must be included on a label. The label must name any fiber that represents more than 5% of the product's weight. The country in which the garment was processed and manufactured must be indicated. Only when clothing is made in the United States and entirely from American materials can it be designated as "Made in the USA."

73. C: It is safe to use bleach on cotton if it is done so occasionally. If bleach is frequently applied to cotton or other cellulosic fibers, the fabric may be damaged. Bleach should not be used on any other fabrics, as it has the ability to cause serious damage. Bleach will often dissolve fabrics made of hair fibers, such as silk, wool, and cashmere. Although bleach can be a valuable tool for fabric cleaning, it must be used sparingly to avoid irreversible damage to fibers.

74. D: Of the given fabrics, black satin would offer the best protection against sunlight. Dark clothing tends to protect the body from ultraviolet radiation better, because they absorb rather than reflect the rays of the sun. Moreover, densely woven fabrics like satin have fewer holes through which sunlight can flow. Of course, black satin might not be the most comfortable fabric to wear in the sun. Dark clothing gets very hot, and sweating in satin clothing can be unpleasant. Many people prefer to wear cotton clothing, because the looser weave allows for superior ventilation. However, cotton offers little protection against UV rays, so it is important to wear sunscreen under the clothing.

75. E: In interior design, the arrangement of elements in a pattern around some central point is known as radial balance. For instance, a dining room might be arranged such that all of the furniture extends out from a central table. The pattern of the radial elements can be based on size, color, or texture. Symmetrical balance is the arrangement of identical elements around a center point or line. This is the most rigidly balanced form of interior design. Gradation balance is the subtle but regular alteration of specific elements in an interior. For instance, a room might include various shades of the same color. Asymmetrical balance is the arrangement of unlike elements that nevertheless creates a balance when looked at as a whole. Harmonic balance is the agreement of the various design elements in a room. It does not entail any particular physical arrangement.

76. B: In a dumbbell layout pattern, spaces are arranged along a linear path, with major elements at either end. This layout pattern is appropriate for houses or buildings in which there are two main places of activity, and it is a good idea to keep the areas separate. A radial layout consists of a number of paths extending out from a central point. This kind of arrangement is typical of offices and buildings with one central purpose. In a clustered layout, several spaces with similar size, shape, and function are grouped close together and linked along a central space or corridor. A doughnut layout, as exemplified by the Pentagon, consists of a circular corridor with rooms on either side. A centralized layout consists of secondary elements arranged around a central point, or axis. One example of a centralized layout is a plaza, in which the central point may be a statue or fountain.

77. A: The Fibonacci sequence, in which each successive number is the sum of the two previous numbers, begins 0, 1, 1, 2, 3, 5. The Fibonacci sequence is one of the classic proportions used frequently in interior design. It occurs often in nature and has been found to be pleasing to the eye. The quantities of the Fibonacci sequence may be numbers of units or distances.

78. C: Housing experts consider air temperature to be the most important determinant of human comfort. There are a number of factors that influence human comfort, but the primary concern for most people with regard to housing is to be kept warm and dry. In general, a house needs to be between 69 and 80 degrees Fahrenheit in order for its inhabitants to be comfortable. The other answer choices are other factors that affect comfort. Relative humidity is the moisture content of the air relative to the amount of moisture that could be in the air at that temperature without condensing. People tend to be comfortable in houses that maintain a relative humidity from 30 to 65%. Mean radiant temperature is the degree to which a person's temperature changes because of radiation. Depending on the air temperature and ventilation of a room, the people and objects within it will either absorb or give off heat. It is more comfortable to absorb heat than to lose it. Air quality is the amount of pollutants and noxious vapors in the atmosphere. Obviously, air quality correlates to comfort. Ventilation is the degree to which the air in a room circulates freely. The amount of ventilation appropriate for a room will depend on its intended use. Kitchens and bathrooms, for instance, tend to benefit from more ventilation.

79. A: Curtains are fabric hung across the window by a rod and cover either the extreme ends of the window or the entire window. The major difference between curtains and draperies is that curtains are hung from a rod and typically lay closer to the window. A louvered shutter is a hard panel in front of a window. The panel consists of one or more planes that can be opened and closed. A grille is a permanent window covering, usually made of metal. Grilles are generally aimed at reducing the amount of light that flows in through a window. A Roman shade is a translucent, accordion-like panel that is raised or lowered with a cord.

80. D: The gross area of the kitchen is 156 square feet. In interior design, the gross area of a room is its area, as well as the areas of any ancillary spaces. Pantries, closets, and similar spaces are considered ancillary. The area of a room is found by multiplying length by width. Sometimes, the length of a pantry or closet will be referred to as depth. If the shape of a space is irregular (for instance, L-shaped), it is best to divide the room into rectangular spaces, find the areas of these spaces, and then add them together.

81. E: Polyester is the synthetic woodwork finish that creates a durable surface. It is an opaque finish, meaning that it obscures the natural look of the lumber underneath. Lacquer, polyurethane, and varnish are the other three popular opaque woodwork finishes. Polyurethane is quite durable as well, but it can be difficult to repair when it is damaged. Varnish can be either opaque or transparent; it is usually easier to apply than lacquer. Vinyl is a transparent finish that is resistant to degradation by moisture and chemicals.

82. B: It is not a good idea to encourage learning-disabled students to strive for perfection. Of course, perfection is an admirable goal, but students with learning disabilities will likely have struggled at times in school and may become discouraged if they fail to reach an impossible standard. Instead, teachers should give students positive reinforcement whenever they make progress. The other answer choices are sound strategies for working with learning-disabled students. Such students can be overwhelmed by complex tasks, even when they are capable of accomplishing each of the constituent steps. Students with learning disabilities thrive when they are given a specific routine for the school day. Such students often become confused and unruly when they do not know what they are supposed to be doing. Students with attention deficit disorder may benefit from lessons that incorporate motion and tactile learning. Because such students often have a surplus of nervous energy, they are better able to focus when they are physically occupied. Finally, dialogue is a great way to introduce abstract concepts to students with learning disabilities. Often, these students need more opportunity to ask questions and receive clarification of difficult concepts.

83. E: The ability to create a personal budget is one of the cognitive objectives of consumer science. Cognitive objectives emphasize intellectual skills, including analysis, synthesis, and evaluation. The creation of a budget requires a student to assemble all information related to income and expenses and to organize that information in a comprehensible table. The abilities to select drapes and restrain consumer impulses are affective objectives, since they require the student to manage his or her emotions and consult his or her taste. The ability to arrange furniture is arguably an affective and psychomotor objective, since it requires physical activity as well as aesthetic sense. The ability to load a shopping cart is a purely psychomotor objective.

84. A: One common criticism of cooperative education programs is that they isolate students from the rest of the academic community. In a cooperative education program, students actually participate in some of the businesses and organizations they are learning about in consumer education class. These programs provide direct on-the-job training and help students make informed career choices later in life. These programs also increase contact between the business and academic communities, which can be rejuvenating for both sectors. Finally, research suggests that cooperative education programs actually increase student motivation, perhaps because they show students the direct application of what they are learning in school.

85. C: Community service is not a focus on Junior Achievement programs at the high school-level. This is not to say that JA programs are indifferent to business ethics. However, the emphasis of Junior Achievement is to prepare students for success in the business community after their education is complete. To this end, the programs administered by JA

focus on economics, personal finance, work preparation, and business and entrepreneurship. Junior Achievement is a non-profit organization that is active in most schools due to the support of corporate and private donations.

86. C: The primary focus of Family, Career, and Community Leaders is the family. Indeed, this is the only in-school student organization that focuses primarily on the family. Since 1945, this organization has worked in all grades to promote the understanding of family roles and responsibilities and to encourage communication between family members and the community at large. Some of the particular points of emphasis for the FCCLA are personal responsibility, community service, and family education.

87. A: A needs assessment for a family and consumer science program should begin with a gap analysis, in which the performance of the class is compared to the performance of students at leading schools. While this may involve a survey of summative assessment results, it should also include a look at the instructional methods, equipment, and community support at the respective schools. This process is similar to the benchmarking performed by business leaders, wherein a business is compared to its most successful competitor. The idea is to bring one's own performance in line with the top performer in one's field. The subsequent needs analysis will define the ways in which the family and consumer science program should improve its approach to leaders in the field.

88. C: A list of community resources is not one of the necessary components of an effective syllabus. A syllabus is essential for organizing the structure and content of a family and consumer science class. Many students do not know what such a course entails, so the syllabus should include a clear mission statement and outline of the course content. The mission statement should state the specific goals of the class. The syllabus should also include clear assessment objectives and an explanation of the grading scale to be used. Experienced teachers know that making the assessment and grading protocols explicit at the beginning of the year can eliminate a great deal of trouble later on.

89. A: Dyssemia is a learning disability that might prevent a student from succeeding in a role-play activity. Dyssemia is a disorder which makes it hard to distinguish social cues and signals. A student with this problem would have a difficult time interpreting the gestures and underlying emotions of his or her fellow participants. Dyssemic students require special instruction about reading another person's body language and vocal tone. Apraxia is a learning disability that inhibits the ability to coordinate movements to accomplish a particular goal. Dysgraphia is associated with difficulty in writing and spelling. Dyslexia is a broad category of language-related learning disabilities that extend beyond reading. Visual perception disorders make it hard for students to identify written words and symbols.

90. E: Of the given factors, an affiliation with the United States government is the least important consideration in the evaluation of Internet research. There are a number of federal government websites that can be valuable for a family and consumer science teacher, but this affiliation is not a guarantee of utility. The Internet can be a great resource for information about family and consumer science, but an educator must ensure that the information obtained online is accurate and from a reputable source. The other four answer choices are factors that should receive consideration when a person is deciding whether a website is credible. Trustworthy websites, especially those connected with universities and

- 113 -

government departments, have an editorial board that approves content. The organization that maintains the website should be easy to discover and investigate. A good website is likely to have links to other, similar websites. Just as we can tell a lot about people by their friends, so we can tell a lot about a site by its links. A trustworthy website will be updated frequently.

91. E: A number of high-school students believe that the most important content area in family and consumer science is food and nutrition. Moreover, this is the most popular family and consumer science subject among high-school students. Perhaps this is because food and nutrition are more relevant to the current lives of high-school students, especially those who are concerned with their physical appearance and health. Housing, family development, and personal finance may not yet be pertinent subjects in the lives of young people. It is incumbent upon the family and consumer sciences teacher, then, to emphasize the importance of these subjects.

92. A: The original purpose of family and consumer science education was to redress social problems such as child labor and the repression of women. In the last years of the nineteenth century, Ellen Swallow Richards convened a group of social reform-minded educators at Lake Placid, New York, to develop programs for domestic economy and household management. These programs were the beginning of what has become family and consumer science education. It is important for teachers to acknowledge that the roots of this subject are in social reform. Even now, the underlying intention of family and consumer science education should be to empower students in their family lives by teaching them to manage their finances and consumer decisions.

93. D: Setting up a mock storefront for a retail business is one way to develop the psychomotor skills of elementary-school students. Psychomotor skills are best acquired through physical action. Setting up a storefront is one such activity, since the best way to learn about product placement is to practice it rather than read or be told about it. Learning to calculate compound interest and looking up banking terms in the dictionary are activities that develop cognitive skills. Drawing a picture of one's ideal house is a good way to develop affective skills. The creation of a budget for a school wardrobe requires a combination of cognitive and affective skills, insofar as the students will need to decide which clothes they want to buy and then work out a comprehensive pricing list.

94. B: One advantage of large classes is that they tend to have greater access to resources. Large classes have more students, and therefore more connections to the community. These connections can be extremely useful in a family and consumer science class. Also, schools are likely to apportion more equipment and financial resources to larger classes. For these reasons, teachers of large classes often have excellent resources at their disposal. The other answer choices are false statements. Large classes tend to create poorer relations between students and teacher, as there are simply too many students for the teacher to establish close relations with each one. Large classes tend to limit the teaching methods that can be used, since some activities are not manageable with a large group. Teachers must keep records for every student, so it stands to reason that larger classes will create more paperwork. Finally, most teachers are more comfortable in an intimate setting with just a few students.

95. A: Experience is not considered a relevant factor when making changes in the family and consumer sciences curriculum. Teachers of all levels of experience should be able to adapt their method and content when called upon to do so. In recent years, there has been pressure for the family and consumer science curriculum to be more closely aligned with general content standards. Teachers do report that knowledge, time, skill, and expense can be significant barriers to change in the curriculum. In particular, many teachers claim that they do not have enough time to implement major changes. The knowledge and skill obstacles may not be the fault of the teacher; for instance, a teacher might not get approval for changes from an administrator who is ignorant about the subject.

96. E: When dividing students up into groups for a project, the best way to avoid gender discrimination is to assign leadership positions to boys and girls in each group. Answer choice D is also a good idea, but it is implicit in answer choice E. Groups should never be segregated by gender unless there is a specific reason for doing so. Also, students should be discouraged from always performing the tasks stereotypically associated with their gender. For example, boys should be encouraged to assume roles related to the arts, while girls should be given opportunities to work with math and science. For most teachers, the best defense against gender discrimination is awareness and a commitment to equal treatment for all students.

97. C: The primary determinant of whether a teacher will adopt instructional technology is perceived usefulness. The cost of the technology is basically irrelevant to the teacher, since it is the school or district that will bear the cost. Student interest is of some importance, since the technology will not be successful unless it is engaging to the students. However, there are plenty of engaging technologies that have little application in the classroom. Geographic location has very little bearing on adoption of technology, since most equipment is available in all parts of the country. Finally, the teacher's aptitude is slightly less important than perceived usefulness, since most teachers assume that they can learn how to use new technologies in a fairly short time.

98. B: The Carl D. Perkins Improvement Act of 2006 mandated that the curriculum of family and consumer science be aligned with general content standards. This act is an offshoot of the No Child Left Behind Act. Its intention is to boost proficiency by ensuring that the content of family and consumer science classes reinforces general academic knowledge. It is part of a general effort to standardize career and technical (formerly known as vocational) education.

99. D: An activity that requires students to describe their ideal home falls within the affective domain. This domain of education encompasses all of the emotional responses to subjects. A child's emotional responses evolve in a manner similar to their intellectual and physical responses. When students are asked to describe his or her ideal house, they are essentially organizing imaginative elements into a coherent response. This management of the imagination is an important skill. The affective domain is one of three outlined in Bloom's taxonomy. The other two are the psychomotor and cognitive domains, concerned with physical and intellectual skills, respectively.

100. E: Between the ages of six and eight, children should develop the ability to count coins. In the first few years of school, children should learn the values of the various coins, and

should be able to assemble different combinations of coins to produce the same value. At this age, children should understand the general purpose of a bank and a savings account. Some children at this age will be able to manage a small allowance. All of the other answer choices are more advanced skills. Making change, comparing prices, maintaining records, and using banking terms are skills not typically developed until at least age nine.

Secret Key #1 - Time is Your Greatest Enemy

Pace Yourself

Wear a watch. At the beginning of the test, check the time (or start a chronometer on your watch to count the minutes), and check the time after every few questions to make sure you are "on schedule."

If you are forced to speed up, do it efficiently. Usually one or more answer choices can be eliminated without too much difficulty. Above all, don't panic. Don't speed up and just begin guessing at random choices. By pacing yourself, and continually monitoring your progress against your watch, you will always know exactly how far ahead or behind you are with your available time. If you find that you are one minute behind on the test, don't skip one question without spending any time on it, just to catch back up. Take 15 fewer seconds on the next four questions, and after four questions you'll have caught back up. Once you catch back up, you can continue working each problem at your normal pace.

Furthermore, don't dwell on the problems that you were rushed on. If a problem was taking up too much time and you made a hurried guess, it must be difficult. The difficult questions are the ones you are most likely to miss anyway, so it isn't a big loss. It is better to end with more time than you need than to run out of time.

Lastly, sometimes it is beneficial to slow down if you are constantly getting ahead of time. You are always more likely to catch a careless mistake by working more slowly than quickly, and among very high-scoring test takers (those who are likely to have lots of time left over), careless errors affect the score more than mastery of material.

Secret Key #2 - Guessing is not Guesswork

You probably know that guessing is a good idea - unlike other standardized tests, there is no penalty for getting a wrong answer. Even if you have no idea about a question, you still have a 20-25% chance of getting it right.

Most test takers do not understand the impact that proper guessing can have on their score. Unless you score extremely high, guessing will significantly contribute to your final score.

Monkeys Take the Test

What most test takers don't realize is that to insure that 20-25% chance, you have to guess randomly. If you put 20 monkeys in a room to take this test, assuming they answered once per question and behaved themselves, on average they would get 20-25% of the questions correct. Put 20 test takers in the room, and the average will be much lower among guessed questions. Why?

1. The test writers intentionally writes deceptive answer choices that "look" right. A test taker has no idea about a question, so picks the "best looking" answer, which is often wrong. The monkey has no idea what looks good and what doesn't, so will consistently be

- 117 -

lucky about 20-25% of the time.

2. Test takers will eliminate answer choices from the guessing pool based on a hunch or intuition. Simple but correct answers often get excluded, leaving a 0% chance of being correct. The monkey has no clue, and often gets lucky with the best choice.

This is why the process of elimination endorsed by most test courses is flawed and detrimental to your performance- test takers don't guess, they make an ignorant stab in the dark that is usually worse than random.

$5 Challenge

Let me introduce one of the most valuable ideas of this course- the $5 challenge:

You only mark your "best guess" if you are willing to bet $5 on it.
You only eliminate choices from guessing if you are willing to bet $5 on it.

Why $5? Five dollars is an amount of money that is small yet not insignificant, and can really add up fast (20 questions could cost you $100). Likewise, each answer choice on one question of the test will have a small impact on your overall score, but it can really add up to a lot of points in the end.

The process of elimination IS valuable. The following shows your chance of guessing it right:

If you eliminate wrong answer choices until only this many remain:	Chance of getting it correct:
1	100%
2	50%
3	33%

However, if you accidentally eliminate the right answer or go on a hunch for an incorrect answer, your chances drop dramatically: to 0%. By guessing among all the answer choices, you are GUARANTEED to have a shot at the right answer.

That's why the $5 test is so valuable- if you give up the advantage and safety of a pure guess, it had better be worth the risk.

What we still haven't covered is how to be sure that whatever guess you make is truly random. Here's the easiest way:

Always pick the first answer choice among those remaining.

Such a technique means that you have decided, **before you see a single test question**, exactly how you are going to guess- and since the order of choices tells you nothing about which one is correct, this guessing technique is perfectly random.

This section is not meant to scare you away from making educated guesses or eliminating choices- you just need to define when a choice is worth eliminating. The $5 test, along with a pre-defined random guessing strategy, is the best way to make sure you reap all of the benefits of guessing.

Secret Key #3 - Practice Smarter, Not Harder

Many test takers delay the test preparation process because they dread the awful amounts of practice time they think necessary to succeed on the test. We have refined an effective method that will take you only a fraction of the time.

There are a number of "obstacles" in your way to succeed. Among these are answering questions, finishing in time, and mastering test-taking strategies. All must be executed on the day of the test at peak performance, or your score will suffer. The test is a mental marathon that has a large impact on your future.

Just like a marathon runner, it is important to work your way up to the full challenge. So first you just worry about questions, and then time, and finally strategy:

Success Strategy

1. Find a good source for practice tests.
2. If you are willing to make a larger time investment, consider using more than one study guide- often the different approaches of multiple authors will help you "get" difficult concepts.
3. Take a practice test with no time constraints, with all study helps "open book." Take your time with questions and focus on applying strategies.
4. Take a practice test with time constraints, with all guides "open book."
5. Take a final practice test with no open material and time limits.

If you have time to take more practice tests, just repeat step 5. By gradually exposing yourself to the full rigors of the test environment, you will condition your mind to the stress of test day and maximize your success.

Secret Key #4 - **Prepare, Don't** Procrastinate

Let me state an obvious fact: if you take the test three times, you will get three different scores. This is due to the way you feel on test day, the level of preparedness you have, and, despite the test writers' claims to the contrary, some tests WILL be easier for you than others.

Since your future depends so much on your score, you should maximize your chances of success. In order to maximize the likelihood of success, you've got to prepare in advance. This means taking practice tests and spending time learning the information and test taking strategies you will need to succeed.

Never take the test as a "practice" test, expecting that you can just take it again if you need to. Feel free to take sample tests on your own, but when you go to take the official test, be prepared, be focused, and do your best the first time!

Secret Key #5 - Test Yourself

Everyone knows that time is money. There is no need to spend too much of your time or too little of your time preparing for the test. You should only spend as much of your precious time preparing as is necessary for you to get the score you need.

Once you have taken a practice test under

real conditions of time constraints, then you will know if you are ready for the test or not.

If you have scored extremely high the first time that you take the practice test, then there is not much point in spending countless hours studying. You are already there.

Benchmark your abilities by retaking practice tests and seeing how much you have improved. Once you score high enough to guarantee success, then you are ready.

If you have scored well below where you need, then knuckle down and begin studying in earnest. Check your improvement regularly through the use of practice tests under real conditions. Above all, don't worry, panic, or give up. The key is perseverance!

Then, when you go to take the test, remain confident and remember how well you did on the practice tests. If you can score high enough on a practice test, then you can do the same on the real thing.

General Strategies

The most important thing you can do is to ignore your fears and jump into the test immediately- do not be overwhelmed by any strange-sounding terms. You have to jump into the test like jumping into a pool- all at once is the easiest way.

Make Predictions

As you read and understand the question, try to guess what the answer will be. Remember that several of the answer choices are wrong, and once you begin reading them, your mind will immediately become cluttered with answer choices designed to throw you off. Your mind is typically the most focused immediately after you have read the question and digested its contents. If you can, try to predict what the correct answer will be. You may be surprised at what you can predict.

Quickly scan the choices and see if your prediction is in the listed answer choices. If it is, then you can be quite confident that you have the right answer. It still won't hurt to check the other answer choices, but most of the time, you've got it!

Answer the Question

It may seem obvious to only pick answer choices that answer the question, but the test writers can create some excellent answer choices that are wrong. Don't pick an answer just because it sounds right, or you believe it to be true. It MUST answer the question. Once you've made your selection, always go back and check it against the question and make sure that you didn't misread the question, and the answer choice does answer the question posed.

Benchmark

After you read the first answer choice, decide if you think it sounds correct or not. If it doesn't, move on to the next answer choice. If it does, mentally mark that answer choice. This doesn't mean that you've definitely selected it as your answer choice, it just means that it's the best you've seen thus far. Go ahead and read the next choice. If the next choice is worse than the one you've already selected, keep going to the next answer choice. If the next choice is better than the choice you've already selected, mentally mark the new answer choice as your best guess.

The first answer choice that you select becomes your standard. Every other answer choice must be benchmarked against that standard. That choice is correct until proven otherwise by another answer choice beating it out. Once you've decided that no other answer choice seems as good, do one final check to ensure that your answer choice answers the question posed.

Valid Information

Don't discount any of the information provided in the question. Every piece of information may be necessary to determine the correct answer. None of the information in the question is there to throw you off (while the answer choices will certainly have information to throw you off). If two seemingly unrelated topics are discussed, don't ignore either. You can be confident there is a relationship, or it wouldn't be included in the question, and you are probably going to have to determine what is that relationship to find the answer.

Avoid "Fact Traps"

Don't get distracted by a choice that is factually true. Your search is for the answer that answers the question. Stay focused and don't fall for an answer that is true but incorrect. Always go back to the question and make sure you're choosing an answer that actually answers the question and is not just a true statement. An answer can be factually correct, but it MUST answer the question asked. Additionally, two answers can both be seemingly correct, so be sure to read all of the answer choices, and make sure that you get the one that BEST answers the question.

Milk the Question

Some of the questions may throw you completely off. They might deal with a subject you have not been exposed to, or one that you haven't reviewed in years. While your lack of knowledge about the subject will be a hindrance, the question itself can give you many clues that will help you find the correct answer. Read the question carefully and look for clues. Watch particularly for adjectives and nouns describing difficult terms or words that you don't recognize. Regardless of if you completely understand a word or not, replacing it with a synonym either provided or one you more familiar with may help you to understand what the questions are asking. Rather than wracking your mind about specific detailed information concerning a difficult term or word, try to use mental substitutes that are easier to understand.

The Trap of Familiarity

Don't just choose a word because you recognize it. On difficult questions, you may not recognize a number of words in the answer choices. The test writers don't put "make-believe" words on the test; so don't think that just because you only recognize all the words in one answer choice means that answer choice must be correct. If you only recognize words in one answer choice, then focus on that one. Is it correct? Try your best to determine if it is correct. If it is, that is great, but if it doesn't, eliminate it. Each word and answer choice you eliminate increases your chances of getting the question correct, even if you then have to guess among the unfamiliar choices.

Eliminate Answers

Eliminate choices as soon as you realize they are wrong. But be careful! Make sure you consider all of the possible answer choices. Just because one appears right, doesn't mean that the next one won't be even better! The test writers will usually put more than one good answer choice for every question, so read all of them. Don't worry if you are stuck between two that seem right. By getting down to just two remaining possible choices, your odds are now 50/50. Rather than wasting too much time, play the odds. You are guessing, but guessing wisely, because you've been able to knock out some of the answer choices that you know are wrong. If you are eliminating choices and realize that the last answer choice you are left with is also obviously wrong, don't panic. Start over and consider each choice again. There may easily be something that you missed the first time and will realize on the second pass.

Tough Questions

If you are stumped on a problem or it appears too hard or too difficult, don't waste time. Move on! Remember though, if you can quickly check for obviously incorrect answer choices, your chances of guessing correctly are greatly improved. Before you completely give up, at least try to knock out a couple of possible answers. Eliminate what you can and then guess at the remaining answer choices before moving on.

Brainstorm

If you get stuck on a difficult question, spend a few seconds quickly brainstorming. Run through the complete list of possible answer choices. Look at each choice and ask yourself, "Could this answer the question satisfactorily?" Go through each answer choice and consider it independently of the other. By systematically going through all

possibilities, you may find something that you would otherwise overlook. Remember that when you get stuck, it's important to try to keep moving.

Read Carefully

Understand the problem. Read the question and answer choices carefully. Don't miss the question because you misread the terms. You have plenty of time to read each question thoroughly and make sure you understand what is being asked. Yet a happy medium must be attained, so don't waste too much time. You must read carefully, but efficiently.

Face Value

When in doubt, use common sense. Always accept the situation in the problem at face value. Don't read too much into it. These problems will not require you to make huge leaps of logic. The test writers aren't trying to throw you off with a cheap trick. If you have to go beyond creativity and make a leap of logic in order to have an answer choice answer the question, then you should look at the other answer choices. Don't overcomplicate the problem by creating theoretical relationships or explanations that will warp time or space. These are normal problems rooted in reality. It's just that the applicable relationship or explanation may not be readily apparent and you have to figure things out. Use your common sense to interpret anything that isn't clear.

Prefixes

If you're having trouble with a word in the question or answer choices, try dissecting it. Take advantage of every clue that the word might include. Prefixes and suffixes can be a huge help. Usually they allow you to determine a basic

- 122 -

meaning. Pre- means before, post- means after, pro - is positive, de- is negative. From these prefixes and suffixes, you can get an idea of the general meaning of the word and try to put it into context. Beware though of any traps. Just because con is the opposite of pro, doesn't necessarily mean congress is the opposite of progress!

Hedge Phrases

Watch out for critical "hedge" phrases, such as likely, may, can, will often, sometimes, often, almost, mostly, usually, generally, rarely, sometimes. Question writers insert these hedge phrases to cover every possibility. Often an answer choice will be wrong simply because it leaves no room for exception. Avoid answer choices that have definitive words like "exactly," and "always".

Switchback Words

Stay alert for "switchbacks". These are the words and phrases frequently used to alert you to shifts in thought. The most common switchback word is "but". Others include although, however, nevertheless, on the other hand, even though, while, in spite of, despite, regardless of.

New Information

Correct answer choices will rarely have completely new information included. Answer choices typically are straightforward reflections of the material asked about and will directly relate to the question. If a new piece of information is included in an answer choice that doesn't even seem to relate to the topic being asked about, then that answer choice is likely incorrect. All of the information needed to answer the question is usually provided for you, and

so you should not have to make guesses that are unsupported or choose answer choices that require unknown information that cannot be reasoned on its own.

Time Management

On technical questions, don't get lost on the technical terms. Don't spend too much time on any one question. If you don't know what a term means, then since you don't have a dictionary, odds are you aren't going to get much further. You should immediately recognize terms as whether or not you know them. If you don't, work with the other clues that you have, the other answer choices and terms provided, but don't waste too much time trying to figure out a difficult term.

Contextual Clues

Look for contextual clues. An answer can be right but not correct. The contextual clues will help you find the answer that is most right and is correct. Understand the context in which a phrase or statement is made. This will help you make important distinctions.

Don't Panic

Panicking will not answer any questions for you. Therefore, it isn't helpful. When you first see the question, if your mind goes blank, take a deep breath. Force yourself to mechanically go through the steps of solving the problem and using the strategies you've learned.

Pace Yourself

Don't get clock fever. It's easy to be overwhelmed when you're looking at a page full of questions, your mind is full of random thoughts and feeling confused, and the clock is ticking down faster than you would like. Calm down and maintain the pace that you have set for yourself. As long as you are on track by monitoring your pace, you are guaranteed to have enough time for yourself. When you get to the last few minutes of the test, it may seem like you won't have enough time left, but if you only have as many questions as you should have left at that point, then you're right on track!

Answer Selection

The best way to pick an answer choice is to eliminate all of those that are wrong, until only one is left and confirm that is the correct answer. Sometimes though, an answer choice may immediately look right. Be careful! Take a second to make sure that the other choices are not equally obvious. Don't make a hasty mistake. There are only two times that you should stop before checking other answers. First is when you are positive that the answer choice you have selected is correct. Second is when time is almost out and you have to make a quick guess!

Check Your Work

Since you will probably not know every term listed and the answer to every question, it is important that you get credit for the ones that you do know. Don't miss any questions through careless mistakes. If at all possible, try to take a second to look back over your answer selection and make sure you've selected the correct answer choice and haven't made a costly careless mistake (such as marking an answer choice that you didn't mean to mark). This quick double check should more than pay for itself in caught mistakes for the time it costs.

Beware of Directly Quoted Answers

Sometimes an answer choice will repeat word for word a portion of the question or reference section. However, beware of such exact duplication – it may be a trap! More than likely, the correct choice will paraphrase or summarize a point, rather than being exactly the same wording.

Slang

Scientific sounding answers are better than slang ones. An answer choice that begins "To compare the outcomes..." is much more likely to be correct than one that begins "Because some people insisted..."

Extreme Statements

Avoid wild answers that throw out highly controversial ideas that are proclaimed as established fact. An answer choice that states the "process should be used in certain situations, if..." is much more likely to be correct than one that states the "process should be discontinued completely." The first is a calm rational statement and doesn't even make a definitive, uncompromising stance, using a hedge word "if" to provide wiggle room, whereas the second choice is a radical idea and far more extreme.

Answer Choice Families

When you have two or more answer choices that are direct opposites or parallels, one of them is usually the correct answer. For instance, if one answer choice states "x increases" and another answer choice states "x decreases" or "y increases," then those two or three answer choices are very similar in construction and fall into the

- 124 -

same family of answer choices. A family of answer choices is when two or three answer choices are very similar in construction, and yet often have a directly opposite meaning. Usually the correct answer choice will be in that family of answer choices. The "odd man out" or answer choice that doesn't seem to fit the parallel construction of the other answer choices is more likely to be incorrect.

Special Report: Additional Bonus Material

Due to our efforts to try to keep this book to a manageable length, we've created a link that will give you access to all of your additional bonus material.

Please visit http://www.mometrix.com/bonus948/priifamconsci to access the information.